Joyce Cary and the Novel of Africa

Joyce Cary and the Novel of Africa

MICHAEL J. C. ECHERUO
University of Nigeria, Nsukka

AFRICANA PUBLISHING COMPANY
NEW YORK

Published in the United States of America 1973
by Africana Publishing Company
Holmes & Meier Publishers, Inc.
101 Fifth Avenue
New York, N.Y. 10003

© Longman Group Ltd 1973

Library of Congress Catalog Card No. 72-76609
ISBN 0–8419–0131–7

for
Kech
who left us at dawn

Printed in Great Britain by
The Camelot Press Ltd, London and Southampton

Contents

Acknowledgements

We are grateful to the following for permission to reproduce copyright material:

Curtis Brown Ltd. and Harper and Row Inc. for extracts from *Aissa Saved, An American Visitor, The African Witch* and *Mister Johnson* by Joyce Cary, ed. Carfax; J. M. Dent and Sons Ltd. and the Trustees of the Joyce Cary Estate for an extract from *Youth, Heart of Darkness and the End of the Tether* by Joseph Conrad; A. D. Peters and Company for an extract from *The Sky and the Forest* by C. S. Forester.

Preface

The present study has grown out of two interests: one an interest in Joyce Cary as a novelist, and the other an interest in the theory of the novel. Both interests met, I think, in 1959 when, as an undergraduate, I first came across Joyce Cary's *Art and Reality*. I was concerned, at that time, with trying to understand how his idea of 'reality' as an aesthetic concept stood in relation to the other 'reality' of his African fiction. Since then I have completed a study of Joyce Cary's major fiction in which I tried to interpret his major European novels in the light of his political, philosophical and aesthetic ideas. When I turned to Cary's African novels, I found that there were special problems which a routine critical analysis was in no position to tackle. In the introductory chapter to the present study, as well as in the short conclusion, I have therefore tried to state some of these problems and to indicate my own way of tackling them.

This study was completed in 1965, but its publication has been unfortunately held up by the Nigerian crisis and war (1967–70). In the years since then, a number of books and critical essays on Joyce Cary's novels have appeared. I have acquainted myself with most of them, and though I do not always say so explicitly in the text, it should be more or less evident that my approach and my conclusions still differ from theirs. I hope that, as a result, I have succeeded in discussing Cary rather than his critics.

My thanks go to Professor A. Mizener of Cornell University who listened to the argument of these essays in more than one form and read the earliest drafts. I should also take this opportunity of expressing my gratitude to Professor M. M.

Mahood (now of the University of Kent at Canterbury) who supervised my undergraduate studies at University College, Ibadan.

University of Nigeria,   MICHAEL J. C. ECHERUO
Nsukka
31 January, 1971

1: The Novel of Africa

To understand and judge Cary's novels of Africa, it is best to begin with a reflection on the tradition of the European or foreign novel of Africa of which they are obviously a part. This is necessary not only because, as will be shown, these four novels betray many of the classical 'weaknesses' associated with European fiction about Africa, but, more importantly, because they give some very clear indications of a departure from that tradition. These novels undoubtedly also belong to the general corpus of Cary's own work and, in that light, also tell the story of his development as a writer. Nevertheless, because they are different from the common run of foreign novels of Africa, these novels have attracted a perhaps undue importance to themselves, especially if they are considered in the context of all of Cary's work. What must, therefore, be recognised is that, these considerations apart, they do occupy a kind of *locus classicus* within the tradition of foreign fiction and that (ironically) they also mark the finest and the very last example of the 'explorer's' novel of Africa. After Cary, it is almost safe to predict, there is not likely again to be another important novel of Africa by a foreigner.

What is the 'foreign novel of Africa' and in what sense is it a special kind of novel? For many readers, the first business of a foreign novel—a novel with an alien setting—is to record, evoke and interpret the life and situation of a foreign people for the education and entertainment of the author's native readers. In this sense, a foreign novel is like a letter home

1

from abroad.[1] The reader is disposed to believe that the facts presented to him are true or essentially so, and that the interpretations based on them are consistent with all the evidence available to the author. In putting so much faith in the authenticity and truth of a foreign novel, the native reader is trying to reassure himself that he has a reliable basis for the responses which are demanded of him by the new and often exotic experiences of the novel. It would thus seem that the general native reader looks to the 'facts' of the story for a basis on which to rest his judgement.

In fact, however, the foreign novel rarely provides the native reader with this basis. More usually, it only offers him a prior evaluation of the evidence. In it, the author, as a kind of folk reporter, uses the distanced peoples and lands of his narrative to make assertions of a large and general kind about human life and human values. The argument of such novels derives its cogency almost entirely from the character and meaning which the author ascribes to the foreign lands and foreign peoples about whom he writes. The episodes may be commonplace, and have their apparent equivalencies in the home setting. But the significance the novel finds in the episodes will usually be founded on an assumed philosophical or moral bias supposedly unique to the environment of action.[2] Accordingly, the valuation of its episodes and of its

[1] See M. M. Mahood, *Joyce Cary's Africa* (London, 1964) which places the 'facts' recorded in Cary's diaries and letters from Africa alongside the 'fiction' that emerged from Cary's African experience. It is as if the fiction was only a transmutation—an artist's transmutation, perhaps—of the letters and diaries. For the present writer, at least, the 'facts' read as strangely as the 'fiction'. See with regard to the connection between the foreign novelist and the 'truth' of his narrative, J. Paul Hunter's 'Friday as a Convert: Defoe and the Accounts of Indian Missionaries', *Review of English Studies*, n.s. 14 (1963), 243–248, and my own '*Robinson Crusoe, Purchas His Pilgrimes* and the "Novel"', in *English Studies in Africa*, X (September 1967), 167–177.

[2] Cf., for example, Harold R. Collins, 'Joyce Cary's Troublesome Africans', *Antioch Review*, XIII (Fall, 1953), 397–406. 'The reader unfamiliar with African affairs may wonder if Cary gives us a trustworthy account of conditions in this important dependency of Britain's Third

characters is determined by an imposed moral code specifically defined for it by the novelist and his cultural assumptions. In such circumstances, the fidelity of reportage becomes of secondary importance to the novelist's overall conception of his foreign context. For it is the difference of this foreign setting from the author's native norm—a continuing and frequently indefinable difference—that constitutes the dominating characteristic of the life of such a novel, and provides the ultimate basis for judgement and criticism.[1]

The foreign novel of Africa is particularly liable to this tendency because it falls back so insistently on a long-standing, highly developed and culturally validated notion of the African scene itself. Thomas Browne's quip about men carrying within them the wonders they seek outside ('there is all Africa and her prodigies in us') only re-echoed an older one about the perpetual mystery of the continent ('*ex Africa aliquid novum*') and anticipates the cruel romance with which the Darwinism of the nineteenth and early twentieth centuries has shrouded the continent. Predictably, then, the European novelist of Africa, at his most serious level, tried to combine in himself the interests of the discoverer and the metaphysician. He recorded the lie of the land and described the patterns of its culture; at the same time he philosophised and moralised on the 'fundamental' meaning of the land and its peoples. Always, at least by implication, he set out to present and explain (that is, 'discover') Africa to his native

Empire. Perhaps he may doubt that Africans are as troublesome and feckless as these novels suggest. Fortunately, it is possible to check this characterisation with the findings of anthropological studies and other authentic non-fiction studies' (p. 397).

[1] David Daiches, *The Novel and the Modern World* (Chicago, 1939), pp. 52–53, speaks of Conrad's 'consistent avoidance of a sophisticated society . . . and of any of the differentia of the modern social world'. Conrad's relation to that world is 'always that of the outsider' and he is only 'successful' when he 'lays his scene in remote parts—the Malay Peninsula, the China Seas' or 'the Carlist salons of Paris in the 1870s', the dim haunts of anarchists in European capitals, the secret intrigue in the curtained-off room'.

3

reader; its mystery, its meaning, its essential distinctiveness.

The emphasis placed here on the native reader is deliberate because it is his shared dispositions with the author and the distance of Africa from both of them that shapes this kind of novel and gives its direction. Whether the author is interested in 'exoticism, reportage or art', to use Dr Ramsaran's categories, his ultimate purpose is to domesticate or at least describe this mystery for his native reader. This means that the European reader approaches the fiction with an attitude of mind vastly different from that with which he reads a novel of Europe. Hence, though it is true, as Miss Mahood says, that Dickens' London was only a reconstitution of the real London,[1] it was nevertheless a reconstitution of a previously recognisable world. And this is why it is possible to detect Dickens' own emphases and to judge his purposes. For Dickens' bleak London scene is a deliberately literary (though vivid) picture of a scene with a thousand other possible significances. The essential meaning of London is not, and was not intended to be, captured in the image that opens *Bleak House*.

A similar comment cannot be made of Conrad's *Heart of Darkness* where place and meaning, fact and impression are said to be (and can only be accepted by the native European reader as being) finally true, 'in essence'. The sombre theme of the novel, Conrad himself said, 'had to be given a sinister resonance, a tonality of its own, a continued vibration that, I hoped, would hang in the air and dwell on the ear after the last note had been struck'.[2] The Congo was his means to this end, and for the native reader this end is perfectly attained in what is, for him, an unforgettable congruence of theme and setting. What the reader might only have suspected as possible (that Africa *is* the heart of darkness), he can now believe as true. For such readers, Conrad succeeds in confirming the old suspicion that Africa (to quote a

[1] Mahood, op. cit., p. 185.

[2] See J. A. Ramsaran, *New Approaches to African Literature*, 2nd ed. (Ibadan, 1970), p. 32.

modern commentator) is the 'symbol of the unpredictable, inscrutable nature of life itself and its challenge to human endeavour. And "a venture to the interior" or "a passage to Africa" ultimately aims at the goal of self-discovery.'[1]

This kind of assertion is a pointer to the force of the influence exerted on the foreign novel of Africa by the base from which it grew. A 'passage to Africa' implies a starting point outside the continent; a 'venture to the interior' presumes a position on its periphery. In effect, the continent is being written about and explored so as to yield a meaning or a significance of interest to the foreign (that is, the European) imagination. The mind it studied was really the European mind; the imagination it finally understood (or delineated) was inevitably the European imagination. But the occasion was conveniently Africa and the various myths of Africa provided the terms of argument and demonstration. If there is anything 'true' of such novels, it is not essentially (or properly) in its setting or in its depiction of character and personality, but in the accuracy of its reflection of the imaginative temper of the author's culture. *Heart of Darkness*, ultimately reveals the mind of an imperial Europe at its day's end; it reveals nothing about the character of Africa itself.

The same conclusion would still be true had Conrad's picture of the Congo been pastoral and Edenic, for in that event, he would still be using such a view of Africa to resolve a contention about the decay of European civilisation by attempting to subvert the old symbol of Africa as hell and a wilderness,[2] and substituting another of it as a tropical Eden. The important difference would have been in the spirit (reluctant or patronising) with which the European imagination would have received the idea of a frankly African utopia. Sidney's *Arcadia*, if we believe Spenser's evidence in *The*

---

[1] Ibid., p. 27.

[2] Cf. Caxton, *Mirror of the World*, ed. Oliver H. Prior, Early English Text Society (Oxford, 1963), p. 94: Africa 'hath his name of helle. . . . In this centre of Ethiope, the peple ben black for hete of the sonne; for it is so hoot in this contre that it semeth that the erthe shold brenne.'

Faerie Queene, was rejected in its own time as 'the abundance of an idle brain':

> [a] painted forgery
> Rather than matter of just memory.

Yet Sidney's evocation of that country is not half as ecstatic and fanciful as this criticism would suggest:

> There were hills which garnished their proud heights with stately trees; humble valleys whose base estate seemed comforted with refreshing of silver rivers; meadows enamelled with all sorts of eye-pleasing flowers; thickets which, being lined with most pleasant shade, were witnessed so to by the cheerful disposition of many well-tuned birds; each pasture stored with sheep feeding with sober security, while the pretty lambs with bleating oratory craved the dame's comfort. Here a shepherd's boy piping, as though he should never be old; there a young shepherdess knitting, and withal singing and it seemed that her voice comforted her hands to work and her hands kept time to her voice's music.[1]

Sir Walter Raleigh's 'factual' account in *The Discovery of Guiana* (1596) is of the same order as Sidney's:

> I never saw a more beautiful country, not more lively prospects; hills so raised here and there over the valleys; the river winding into divers branches, the plains adjoining without bush or stubble; all fair green grass, the ground of hard sand easy to march on, either for horse or foot; the deer crossing in every path; the birds towards the evening singing on every tree with a thousand several tunes; cranes and herons of white, crimson and carnation perching on the river's side; the air fresh with a gentle easterly wind, and every stone that we stopped to take up promised either gold or silver by his complexion.[2]

The true interest in both Sidney's 'fictional' account and in Raleigh's 'true' report is in their philosophic prejudice, their picture of a new Elysium. Both are shot through with images of an earthly paradise modelled on a conflation of

[1] This passage is taken for convenience from *Elizabethan and Jacobean Prose, 1550–1620*, ed. Kenneth Muir, Pelican Book of English Prose, Vol. I (London, 1956), pp. 160–161. The text has been modernised.

[2] Ibid., p. 35.

tropical and temperate pastures,[1] of the Golden age of the pagan world and the mythic garden of the Jewish Testament. Both authors give us a similar utopia because their philosophical or propagandist bias led them to it, inevitably.

This bias or predisposition, whether high-minded or petty, is central to all foreign fiction. It determines the selection, ordering and interpretation of evidence. Without it, Sidney's would have become a Dorset countryside overpraised; without it, foreign lands and peoples will lose all their interest and cogency for the reader. Melville, who himself detested the simple graphic black and white symbolism of his age, also understood this and beautifully undermines this convention in *Redburn*. His hero-narrator, Redburn, is on his first trip to Liverpool.

> At last, one morning. I came on deck, and they told me that Ireland was in sight.
>
> Ireland in sight! A foreign country actually visible! I peered hard, but could see nothing but a bluish, cloud-like spot to the northeast. Was that Ireland? Why, there was nothing remarkable about that; nothing startling. If *that's* the way a foreign country looks, I might as well have stayed at home.
>
> Now what exactly I had fancied the shore would look like, I cannot say; but I had a vague idea that it would be something strange and wonderful. However, there it was and as the light increased and the ship sailed nearer and nearer, the land began to magnify, and I gazed at it with increasing interest.
>
> Ireland! I thought of Robert Emmet, and that last speech of his before Lord Norbury; I thought of Tommy Moore, and his amatory verses; I thought of Burran, Grattan, Plunket, and O'Connell; I thought of my uncle's ostler, Patrick Flinnigan; and I thought of the shipwreck of the gallant *Albion*, tost to pieces on the very shore now in sight; and I thought I should very much like to leave the ship and visit Dublin and the Giant's Causeway.[2]

[1] Guiana's 'weather', according to Raleigh, is 'extreme hot, the river bordered with very high trees that kept away the air. Sidney's Arcadia, on the other hand, is a temperate country with 'stately trees', 'meadows' and 'thickets . . . lined with most pleasant shade'. *Elizabethan and Jacobean Prose*, pp. 34, 160.

[2] Herman Melville, *Redburn, His First Voyage*, Anchor ed. (New York, 1957), pp. 117–118.

One is not, of course, denying that it is legitimate to use a landscape for symbolic purposes. Melville himself was to do this so well in *Benito Cereno*. There is, in any event, a long tradition of this association of setting and meaning in European literature. This would include not only the linking of sentiment and action to a significant landscape or landmark (as in much heroic poetry) but also the full-scale exploitation of landscape for naturalistic, symbolic or even 'Gothic' purposes. The use of the African setting for clearly symbolic functions can, in this sense, be said to be an extension of this tradition. There is this difference, however: that unlike its counterpart from the 'home country', the African setting carries with it an axiomatic and automatic signification; that the setting is presumed to be in some way a mere externalisation of a meaning peculiarly African and foreign.

Accordingly, we have in the foreign novel, a confirmation of an attitude rather than an exploration of possibilities of meaning. In *Wuthering Heights*, as well as in *The Return of the Native* (to use two popular examples), there is a tender imaginative harmony between the psychological and moral tensions of the novels and the weird, overwhelming and tyrannous world outside. The effect is to deepen the intensity of the message, not to diagnose or characterise the setting. But in a foreign novel, in *Heart of Darkness* for example, every detail of description re-echoes a positive and culturally responsible prejudice. Conrad describes the air above Gravesend as 'dark . . . and farther back still seemed condensed into a mournful gloom, brooding motionless over the biggest and the greatest town on earth'. But the description is only a mood of the moment. It only reflects the extent of the deterioration (which Conrad is anxious to state) of the Thames from its pristine quality as 'venerable', 'serene', 'less brilliant but more profound'.

> The old river in its broad reach rested unruffled at the decline of day, after ages of good service done to the race that peopled its banks, spread out in the tranquil dignity of a waterway leading to the uttermost ends of the earth. . . . Hunters of gold or pursuers of

> fame, they all had gone out on that stream, bearing the sword, and
> often the torch, messengers of the might within the land, bearers of
> the sacred fire. What greatness had not floated on the ebb of that
> river into the mystery of an unknown earth![1]

This Thames scene, then, only provokes a kind of momentary, though disturbing, gloom. In reality it is only a prefiguration of the more truly disturbing 'mystery' of the 'unknown earth' of the Congo River: 'a mighty big river resembling an immense snake uncoiled, with its head in the sea, its body at rest curving afar over a vast country, and its tail lost in the depths of the land' (p. 52). This image, a reversal of the Edenic model of the river of life, is not an accidental one. The image of a primordial, but post-lapsarian Africa fits beautifully into the neat schemes which wanted to make Africa the physical equivalent of the 'uncanny', 'fateful' and blighted soul of a destructive imperialism. The Congo and the disease of exploitative European imperialism can thereby become one.

> We called at some places with farcical names, where the merry
> dance of death and trade goes on in a still and earthly atmosphere
> as of an overheated catacomb, all along the formless coast bordered
> by dangerous surf as if Nature herself tried to ward off intruders;
> in and out of rivers, streams of death in life, whose banks were
> rotting into mud, whose waters, thickened into slime, invaded the
> contorted mangroves, that seemed to writhe at us in the extremity
> of an impotent despair. . . . It was like a weary pilgrimage amongst
> hints for nightmares (p. 62).

Heart of Darkness is too lyrical a record of impressions, perhaps, to be representative of the manner of most European novels of Africa which try, in the tradition of Defoe's *Captain Singleton*, to give the impression of fact and circumstance about the continent. Yet the ends of Conrad's kind of novel are the same as theirs: the use of Africa as a kind of *persona* in the fiction and the conversion of the environment

[1] Joseph Conrad, *Heart of Darkness*, in *Youth, Heart of Darkness and The End of the Tether*, Everyman ed. (London, 1967), pp. 45, 46, 47. Subsequent page references to *Heart of Darkness* will be given in parentheses after the text.

into a character. It involves a prejudgement of every event taking place against the back-drop of the African continent; it argues for a predetermination of the life of Africa resulting from a view of the nature of Africa itself.[1]

The consequence of all this is that fidelity to detail and truthfulness of report cease to be relevant critical considerations. In *Heart of Darkness*, it is totally irrelevant to consider the details of description in the light of any so-called 'facts' of the Congo. This is so because the narrative prejudice is more important than the narrated fact:

> (a) Now and then a boat from the Shore gave one a momentary contact with reality. It was paddled by black fellows. You could see from afar the white of their eyeballs glistening. They shouted, sang; their bodies streamed with perspiration; they had faces like grotesque masks—these chaps; but they had bone, muscle, a wild vitality, an intense energy of movement, that was as natural and true as the surf along the coast. They wanted no excuse for being there (p. 61).

> (b) A rocky cliff appeared, mounds of turned-up earth by the shore, houses on a hill, there with iron roofs, amongst a waste of excavations, or hanging to the declivity. A continuous noise of the rapids alone hovered over this scene of inhabited devastation. A lot of people, mostly black and naked, moved about like ants. A jetty projected into the river. A blinding sunlight drowned all this at times in a sudden recrudescence of glare (p. 63).

In these passages, the picture is clear and the narrative tone of voice unequivocal. What this voice establishes is a mood and an attitude, and these, in turn, colour the vision including the facts.

By narrative prejudice, then, we mean that total and powerful ascription of a definite moral character to event and location; we mean that complex of fact and attitude which makes the people, the jungles, the rivers, the crocodiles—

[1] My argument here goes beyond what Dr E. N. Obiechina has called Europe's 'near-rejection of the human integrity of the African and a questioning of the autonomy of the African way of life'. See his article, 'Through the Jungle Dimly: European Novelists on West Africa', in *Literary Studies* (Punjab, India), I (Fall, 1970), pp. 113–123.

even the rain and sun of Africa—the permanent symbols of a dark and violent mystery. Against this background, it would be as idle to argue about the correspondence of Conrad's Congo to the true Congo as it would be to establish the original model for Sycorax's magic island.

The point being made is that for European novelists, Africa is not only a place but a moral influence. For almost all of them, it is a reversal of Eden, lush and fruitful but lacking the benefit of redemption from the serpent. In their view, this Africa has a specifically debilitating moral influence. In the case of Conrad's Kurtz, this Africa took on him 'a terrible vengeance for the fantastic invasion' (p. 131). This Africa is the 'heartless mistress' of Florence Kilpatrick's *Red Dust*, a 'mistress' which 'cruelly flouted [the white men] when their hopes ran highest'.[1]

In the romances and jungle novels, it is the burden of the white man to triumph over this Africa in all its manifestations. And this is, ultimately, responsible for the extensive, exotic and fanciful accounts of physical conditions in Africa; for the celebration of those details that would not only glorify the achievement of the pioneers in conquest but also, as it were, recapture some of the mysterious charm which provoked and justified the adventure in the first place. In the more serious novels, Africa becomes the spiritual wilderness through which the European hero has to pass on his way to redemption. Altogether, the physical fact of Africa is subsumed in the simple moral symbol with which it is only accidentally (that is, by the accident of European intellectual history) associated.

It is easy, therefore, to see why there is so much moral earnestness in the more serious European novels of Africa; why the action seems always to take a deterministic and fatal turn, and why, otherwise fanciful performances like C. S. Forester's *The Sky and the Forest* can assume the character of serious, even important, fiction. In Forester's novel, the

[1] See G. D. Killam, *Africa in English Fiction, 1874–1939* (Ibadan, 1968), p. 3.

spiritual values of Loa and his fellow kinsmen of Equatorial Africa are founded on the ruling influence of forest and sky.

> Now the trees suddenly began to be farther apart, the leaf-mould underfoot suddenly became firmer, and the path took a steeply upward slope. For a few moments it was a steep climb. The forest ended abruptly here, where the soil changed to naked rock on which even in that bush atmosphere nothing could grow. They were out of the forest and under the sky, and a few more strides took them to the top of the rock, looking over the vast river. Loa did not like this. He was inclined to flinch a little as he emerged from the forest. The sky was his brother but an unfriendly brother, a frightening brother. He did not like great spaces.[1]

Loa's movement from forest to open ground is, symbolically, a momentary and involuntary escape from the throes of his jungle hell. Forester insists on this meaning throughout the novel and makes the forest the source of all the evil of the novel's action:

> The forest provided almost no meat. . . . The best meat the forest afforded walked on two legs; the African forest was one of the few places in the world where cannibalism was an economic necessity, where it was indulged in to appease an irresistible, an insatiable hunger for meat (p. 11).

The forest, too, is literally in a state of civil disorder:

> In the forest there was always going on a silent life and death struggle for light and air, even for rain. Every plant depended on these three, pushed and aspired and strove to out-top its neighbours, to gain elbow room where it could spread out in the life-giving light and air. In the virgin forest the victors in the struggle were the trees. . . .
>
> If a big tree paid the penalty for its very success by being selected to be struck by lightning, or if it had died of old age, or if a forest fire had killed trees over a large area, and more especially where man had cut down trees for his own purposes, light and air would penetrate to earth level, and the lowly plants had their opportunity which they grasped with feverish abandon. The clearing became a battle ground of vegetation. . . . It would be a long struggle, but as

[1] C. S. Forester, *The Sky and the Forest* (London, 1948), p. 66. Subsequent page references to this novel will be given in parentheses after quotations.

> the year passed the trees would assert their mastery more and more
> forcibly; the undergrowth would die away, the fallen trees would rot
> to powder, and in the end the clearing would be indistinguishable
> from the rest of the forest, silent and dark (pp. 12–13).

It is to this 'silent and dark' forest that Loa prays at one
of the key moments of crisis as he searches for his dear
Musini and Lanu who are held captive.

> He was as near to the pen as he could ever get unobserved. . . . The
> sun blazed down into the undergrowth around him so that he was in
> a steady trickle of sweat; insects plagued him and hunger and thirst
> assailed him, but he forced himself to lie there waiting; he called to
> his assistance all the endless patience of the forest (pp. 127–128).

In the context of Forester's rhetoric in the novel, 'patience'
here is hardly a virtue; in fact it represents the characteristic
of the Congo itself. For a thousand years 'at least', the novel
says, 'perhaps for many thousand years, the forest and its
people had lain in torpor and peace', which 'the Arab
invasions' were to change, destroying 'the equilibrium of the
life in the deep central recesses of the forest' (p. 185). Hence
Loa's rise and fall at the hands of the Arabs and then the
Belgians is symbolic of the penetration and conquest of
aboriginal Africa by the soldiers of Reason and Light. The
darkness and ignorance in Loa's head as well as the violence
of action around him find their counterpart in the necessary
primitive violence of the African forest itself. At the end of the
novel when Loa and his wife are shot to death, the darkness,
as it were, clears and the forest is ready to yield to the light
of the open sky of European civilisation under King Leopold
of the Belgians!

The question that is not often asked is whether Forester's
very confident assertion of these correspondences is even good
enough reason to hold them as possibly true. This is the
fundamental weakness of the criticism of the European novel
of Africa: that the commentators appear to give prompt
assent to the novelist's thesis and proceed to generalise on
Africa and Africans in the light of such theses. G. D. Killam,
for example, argues that the 'moral issue at stake' in Francis

Brett Young's *The Crescent Moon*, ('a contest between "good" and "evil"') 'redeems to some extent the improbabilities which are inherent in the structure of the plot'. He concludes:

> Young manages to suggest, *strongly and plausibly*, not only that 'Africa was a wholly savage land, . . . a land above all others, which men of European race had never conquered', but also that the 'huge and sinister back-ground . . . so vast and sombre . . . against which human figures very small and distant struggling [*sic*] with feeble limbs, incapable of controlling their destinies' was symbolic of the human condition.[1]

Such a symbolic meaning must be assumed to derive from the European imagination rather than intrinsically from the African environment; to represent the cultural dilemma of a questing European mind rather than the doom of a so-called savage African reality. The distinction is real.

In any event, this attitude to Africa explains also the use of the continent as an expiatory symbol. Just as men fled from the world to the monastery, from the city to the countryside, from battlefields to libraries, from sin to redemption, so they moved from Europe to Africa in search of a different kind of life. The mere movement was enough symbolism in itself. And just as William Golding's choirboys moved from London into the jungle of primordial corruption, brutality and eventual redemption, so the heroes of these novels moved into Africa to face their initial penance or baptism. In these novels, expatriation when involuntary became a kind of pilgrimage and ordeal, but became salutary when undertaken voluntarily, as a gesture of revolt from Europe. Indeed, most of the European novels of Africa in which European characters play a major role have one common theme: the re-education of the white man in the jungle-purgatory of Africa. It is with the anxieties, expectations, frustrations and fulfilment of the European man in the alien world of Africa that these novels are concerned.

In the more directly colonial novels concerned with

[1] *Africa in English Fiction*, p. 13.

14

governors, soldiers, traders and missionaries, these issues are dealt with as the inevitable consequences of a moral responsibility to Africa and the African. In quite a number of other sophisticated novels, however, in Romain Gary's *The Roots of Heaven*, for example, the choice of Africa and its adventures is a calculated act of atonement, a deliberate gesture towards the salvation of the self. Gary's hero, Morel, is disillusioned by the warped and exhausted nature of European civilisation and by the excruciating experiences of war. He finds his ideal of peace and fulfilment in a romantic identification with the wild elephants of the African jungle. As one of the characters says, Morel was a man who 'had gone even further in loneliness than others'.

> —and that's a real exploit, by the way; for where breaking records in loneliness is concerned we're all champions in the field. Morel often comes to visit during my sleepless nights, with that angry look of his and the three deep lines on his straight, obstinate forehead, under the shock of hair, and carrying his famous brief-case which never left him even in the jungle; and I often hear him repeating to me, in that rather common voice of his, so unexpected in a man who has received, as we say, an education:
> 'You see, dogs aren't enough any more. People feel damn lonely, they need company, they need something bigger, stronger, to lean on, something that can really stand up to it all. Dogs aren't enough: what we need is elephants.'[1]

Morel was shattered by the experiences of life in European concentration camps. As a result he 'hated his fellow men' and was becoming 'like a rogue elephant who attacks any one in sight' (p. 11). His mission in Africa—to protect the elephants of Chad from extinction at the hands of tusk-hunters—is consequently both high-minded and bestial: 'an extreme case of misanthropy and also a lone fight for the dignity of man' (p. 12), as the novel puts it.

The Roots of Heaven is, in consequence, an elaborate parable

---

[1] Romain Gary, *The Roots of Heaven*, Penguin ed. (London, 1960), p. 11. Subsequent references will be given in parentheses. Originally published as *Les Racines du Ciel* (Librairie Gallimard, 1956), *The Roots of Heaven* was first issued in English in 1958 by Michael Joseph.

15

using the French Colony of Chad as a sufficiently distanced and conveniently foreign setting. Europe had to have its contrast in Africa, and Morel his fulfilment there. At the moment of confrontation between Morel and the local authorities, the world of Africa, seen in its primary contrasts with that of Europe, appears in its most mystical and portentous dimensions.

> The sun had just gone down into the forest, and every bush, every tree seemed to be sharing in its scarlet spoils. As we moved slowly, a sound like thunder rose towards us from the banks of the Galandale, the whole forest seemed to shake and yield under some furious assault and the air and the sky itself were filled with the trumpeting of the herd as it blazed its way towards water; in a few moments the cracking of uprooted trees, the trembling of the earth and rocks and the calls of the elephants took on the proportions of some natural cataclysm. I listened. I was used to it, and yet every time, that living thunder made my heart beat faster, and it wasn't fear, but a strange contagion (p. 113).

The novel links this crucial movement of the elephants with the 'strange contagion' of Africa. The scene leads insistently to wider and larger conclusions: to the fear that 'soon there will be no more room in the modern world for such a need of space, for such a royal clumsiness, such magnificent freedom'; to the conviction that 'in this age of impotence . . . we had not yet finally cut off from our sources, that we had not yet been once and for all castrated and enslaved, that we were not yet altogether subdued'. This moment of illumination is also, according to the novel's thesis, one of justification for Morel. It was hard, the narrator confesses, 'very hard . . . not to take one's place at Morel's side' (p. 113).

Looked at quite closely, Morel's position is fundamentally Darwinian. It is an extension of the old evolutionary argument to that sublime level where Africa the mysterious and wild merges with Africa the unchanging and original birthplace of man.

> 'It must be amusing to be killed at my age!
> 'Hilarious,' I assured him. 'How old are you?'

16

'I am very old,' he said gravely.

He added as a matter of course: 'I'm glad to die in Africa.'

'And why?'

'Because this is where mankind began. The cradle of humanity is in Nyasaland. . . . One dies better at home.'

Yet another one, I thought, who's trying to find a home on earth (p. 114).[1]

The meaning, then, of *The Roots of Heaven* is human and European rather than African. The concerns which the jungles and elephants are used to discuss are European and foreign. Africa is only an attractive and convenient expedient which, as Waitari, the African nationalist of the novel says, nevertheless remains the slum of the world. 'Every lion, every elephant at liberty means still more waiting and still more savagery and primitivism. . . . Africa will never awake to her destiny until she has stopped being the world's zoo' (pp. 294–295). The final lesson which the Jesuit missionary derives from Morel's adventure is, rightly enough, a reflection on the Europe that had lost its moral stability and its self-confidence after the atrocities of Auschwitz and the Second World War.[2] As the Jesuit came to understand it, this lesson was to be found in the words of Saint-Denis who saw Morel's task as complementary to the Jesuit's search for Grace. 'I prefer to believe that you are not untouched by a certain secret sympathy for that rebel, whose idea is to

---

[1] It is interesting to read Robert Ardrey's *African Genesis* (1961) as an extended commentary on the argument of this passage. 'Not in innocence, and not in Asia, was mankind born. The home of our fathers was the African highland reaching north from the Cape to the Lakes of the Nile. Here we came about—slowly, ever so slowly—on a sky-swept savannah glowing with menace.' Collins ed. (London, 1967), p. 7.

[2] See Ardrey, *African Genesis* (p. 32) for the author's thoughts on seeing the baby jaw bone of the Makapan *Australopithecus Africanus* broken, according to all available evidence, by a violent stroke. 'I understood his conviction that the predatory transition and the weapons fixation explained man's bloody history, his eternal aggression, his irrational, self-destroying inexorable pursuit of death for death's sake. . . . Would it be wise for us to listen when man at last possessed weapons capable of sterilizing the earth?'

17

extract from Heaven itself this minimum of respect for our condition. After all, our race emerged from the mud some millions of years ago, and although we got rid of our scales, there is still a long way to go before we become really human' (pp. 363–364). To say of this lesson that it is 'human' is not to mean that it is also 'African'.

Yet it ought to be stressed that the evolutionary hypothesis which stands behind the words of Saint-Denis, though it has given strength and definition to the European fictional exploration of the idea of Africa, has also led it into grave errors and indiscretions. Two of these may be mentioned by way of illustration. The first is the temptation to represent Africa merely as a manifestation of these habits of barbarism beyond which the European mind has progressed. The novelists accordingly fall back on the conclusions of European anthropologists on the place of myth and sacrifice in primitive' societies; they adopt the psychologists' explanation of the nature of 'primitive man' and of the Freudian and Jungian demons that can so furiously impel him. Conrad's little starving African criminal ('the man seemed young—almost a boy—but you know with them it's hard to tell') tied a 'bit of white worsted round his neck' in a way that made conjecture inevitable. 'Was it a badge—an ornament—a charm—a propitiatory act? Was there an idea at all connected with it? It looked startling round his black neck, this bit of white thread from beyond the seas' (p. 67). Deeper 'into the heart of darkness'. Conrad's narrator finds the natural 'peace' broken up at night by the roll of drums behind the curtain of trees.

> Whether it meant war, peace, or prayer we could not tell . . . We were wanderers on prehistoric earth, on an earth that wore the aspect of an unknown planet. We could have fancied ourselves the first of men taking possession of an accursed inheritance, to be subdued at the cost of profound anguish and of excessive toil. But suddenly . . . there would be a glimpse of rush walls, a whirl of black limbs, a mass of hands clapping, of feet stamping, of bodies swaying, of eyes rolling, under the droop of heavy and motionless foliage. The steamer toiled along slowly on the edge of a black and incomprehen-

sible frenzy. The prehistoric man was cursing us, praying to us, welcoming us—who could tell? (pp. 95–96).

Among such people, what hope! 'I don't think a single one of them had any clear idea of time, as we at the end of countless ages have. They still belonged to the beginning of time—had no inherited experience to teach them as it were' (p. 103). In *Heart of Darkness* there is a kind of sustained poetic flourish to this representation which, when accepted, gives the performance its mysterious and solemn dignity. It is this solemnity, after all, that makes it possible for Conrad to merely hint at Kurtz's participation in 'certain midnight dances ending with unspeakable rites' (p. 118), while elsewhere speaking grandly of the wilderness that had 'taken' Kurtz, 'loved him, embraced him, got into his veins, consumed his flesh, and sealed his soul to its own by the inconceivable ceremonies of some devilish initiation' (p. 115).

In Forester's *The Sky and the Forest*, the representation of primitive Africa is rather direct and embarrassingly bald, because the poetic flourishes are so clearly absent. In the Africa of this novel, men are ruled by what Forester calls instincts: 'the sensitive instincts of an uneducated man'.

> [Loa] did not have to follow along the path of deduction and logic, from the fact that Indeharu and Vira were carefully refraining from exchanging glances, to the fact that their expressions were unnaturally composed, and then on to the fact that Vira bore an old grudge against Soli . . . and from that to this knowledge of Indeharu's enmity towards Soli . . . Loa's instincts leaped all the gaps without any painful building of bridges (p. 8).

According to the novel, Loa was incapable of logical thought for two reasons. First he 'had never been under the necessity of thinking logically'. Secondly, he 'was handicapped by his language, which with its clumsy complexities of construction and its total want of abstract terms was not an instrument adapted to argument or for the conveyance of more than the simplest ideas. His mind was much more a meeting ground for conveying impulses' (p. 12). And in a further piece of extended analysis, the novel explains that

'even if the forest people had learned to write, their language
—the clumsy, complicated, unimproved language of the
barbarian—was enough to hamper thoughts and impede
their diffusion.'

> Thought is based on words, and Loa's words were few and simple yet
> linked together—tangled would be a better term—by a grammar of
> unbelievable clumsiness. And Loa lived in a climate where there
> were no seasons, where the nights were hardly less warm than the
> days, where it was easy to do nothing—as Loa was doing now;
> where there was no need to take thought for the morrow—and Loa
> was taking none (pp. 26–27).

Once this idea of the 'primitive' African mind is accepted,
a second error becomes inevitable: the representation of the
transitional African as a tragically absurd and pitiable
character. G. D. Killam, in his study of the problem, complains that 'the most imaginative novelists—those whose
sympathies are widest and whose adjustment of character,
situation and setting to the demands of fiction are most
successful—allow themselves to be controlled by pressures
outside the realm of fiction—that is, the intellectual and
social climate which caused them to present both the primitive and the educated African characters in a consistently
unrealistic convention'.[1] The 'educated African' who 'might
have been expected to symbolise African advancement'
becomes 'a despised and unsympathetic character'.[2] There
is really no reason for surprise. The idea of a primitive
African—the African of Forester's imagination, for example
—depends on an assumed harmony between the man and his
environment; it also assumes that the direction and momentum of evolutionary growth for the African were different
from those of the European.[3] The intermixture of a 'primitive'

[1] G. D. Killam, *Africa in English Fiction, 1874–1939*, pp. 80–81.

[2] Ibid., p. 71.

[3] Cf. Harold R. Collins, op. cit., p. 405: 'Even if we admit that the
Africans are childish in an absolute sense because they are nurtured in a
less sophisticated culture founded on prescientific, irrational, childlike
thought, we must admit also that they are not staying in that stage of
human development.'

mind and a 'progressive' European mental attitude was, on these grounds, bound to produce an absurdity, whether tragic or comic. One prejudice breeds another.

In *The Sky and the Forest*, Forester happily excludes this class of character from the world of Africa. His Africans are instead the original natives whose careers, accordingly, run the grand and primitive course of violence and death. The brave Lanu dies from a direct bullet wound during his daring raid on the *Lady Stanley* commanded by Captain Talbot. And Loa himself refused to die a mean and unworthy death. Talbot had hoped to use him 'as a local under-governor' who would help him 'to organise the district of rubber collecting and ivory hunting' (p. 218). Loa thought otherwise. With 'the pitiless sky overhead looking down at him' and 'the friendly forest far away', he decided to make his last god-like gesture of defiance:

> At the last moment, Loa sprang, whirling back the axe for a last blow.
> But the stiffness of his fifty years betrayed him; he could not leap fast enough to catch the white man entirely off his guard. Talbot just managed to leap aside, in a most undignified fashion, without even time enough to pull the trigger. But the rifle of the kneeling escort had followed Loa's movements, and the bullet struck Loa in the side as he poised on one foot with the axe above his head. From side to side the heavy bullet tore through him, from below upwards, expanding as it went. It struck him below the ribs on his right side. It pierced his liver, it tore his heart to shreds, and, emerging, it shattered his left arm above the elbow. So Loa died in that very moment, the axe dropping behind him as he fell over with a crash (pp. 218–219).

In *Heart of Darkness*, Conrad is too occupied with Marlow and Kurtz to deal with this phenomenon of the transitional African in detail. But he does speak early in the novel of an African guard as 'one of the reclaimed, the product of the new forces at work'.

> [He] strolled despondently, carrying a rifle by its middle. He had a uniform jacket with one button off, and seeing a white man on the path, hoisted his weapon to his shoulder with alacrity. This was

21

simple prudence, white men being so much alike at a distance that he could not tell who I might be. He was speedily reassured, and with a large, white rascally grin and glance at his charge seemed to take me unto partnership in his exulted trust. After all, I also was a part of the great causes of these high and just proceedings (pp. 64–65).

Similarly, the ship's fireman is an early product of the new disruption of Africa's primitive ways. 'He was an improved specimen; he could fire up a vertical boiler.'

> He was there below me, and, upon my word, to look at him was as edifying as seeing a dog in a parody of breeches and a feather hat, walking on his hind legs. A few months of training had done for that really fine chap (p. 97).

This unnamed fireman, we are told, 'squinted at the steam-gauge and at the water-gauge with an evident effort of intrepidity—and he had filed teeth, too, the poor devil, and the wool on his pate shaved into queer patterns, and three ornamental scars on each of his cheeks'.

> He ought to have been clapping his hands and stamping his feet on the bank, instead of which he was hard at work, a thrall to strange witchcraft, full of improving knowledge. He was useful because he had been instructed and what he knew was this—that should the water in that transparent thing disappear, the evil spirit inside the boiler would get angry through the greatness of his thirst, and take a terrible vengeance. So he sweated and fired up and watched the glass fearfully (with an impromptu charm, made of rags, tied to his arm, and a piece of polished bone, as big as a watch, struck flat-ways through his lower lip) (pp. 97–98).

Conrad's fireman is a long way from the more sophisticated and more complicated 'educated' Africans of the European novel of Africa. What he has in common with them is an absurd existence between the assumed terrors and innocent simple-mindedness of the past and the dynamic and complex experience of a Europeanised present. It was in the nature of his condition that he should be a comic (and potentially tragic) embarrassment to himself—a 'dog in a parody of breeches and a feather hat, walking on his hind legs', as Conrad phrased it.

Hence it is that Cary's Bible-quoting Ojo (of *Aissa Saved*),

22

the Wordsworth-quoting Oxford graduate, Aladai (of *The African Witch*) and the petty clerk, Johnson (of *Mister Johnson*) belong to a long and honoured tradition of African characters of European fiction. To a large extent, the absurdity of their roles in the fiction approximated the operatic clumsiness of their actual counterparts in real life.[1] Yet the significance of this kind of character went beyond verisimilitude. It represented a symbolic affirmation of an established point of view which saw the whole movement of ideas and events in Africa as essentially tragic though comic in its external appearance. The educated characters, therefore, labour under the unusual and insurmountable handicap of not being capable, in any circumstances, of changing either themselves or their continent. Dr Craven's hope (in Mary Gaunt's *The Silent Ones*) of bringing 'the past of Africa out of darkness into light', and of giving it 'a place in the history of the world'[2] is as doomed as the hopeless dream republic of Cary's Aladai (*The African Witch*). And this failure is made all the more remarkable by the fact that both men had all the opportunity and all the education Europe gave to the very best of her own sons; for Craven, Cambridge (Natural Science Tripos, Medicine) and Heidelberg (Medicine, under the eminent Professor Schon); for Aladai, Oxford (Political Thought and Modern History).

[1] For a contemporary picture of the cultural situation in nineteenth-century Africa, the Lagos press of the period is invaluable. See, for example: *Lagos Weekly Record*, 2 July 1892 ('A Novelty for a Dull London Season'); 20 September 1892 (Blyden's paper to the Swedenborg Society on 'England and the Black Race'); 1 October 1892 (on a Western-style wedding at Bonny); 14 October 1893 (on 'The Education of Children in England'); 14 April 1894 (on the problems of African Youth); 27 June 1895 (on 'The Negro and European Civilization'); 21 September 1895 (for 'An Indictment of the Negro'); 21 December 1895 (on Europe's task of 'Civilizing Africa'); 21 March 1896 (on 'Yoruba literature as a Desideratum' and on 'Native Institutions'); 15 August 1896 (for a fictionalised 'European View of Civilized Social life in Lagos'); 24 October 1896 (on 'The Aboriginal Native in British Colonies') and 5 December 1896 (on 'Heathenish Native Customs').

[2] See Killam, p. 74.

Commenting on Craven's death 'just when he is achieving his quest', Killam describes the treatment of the principal character as 'melodramatic'. Such a denouement, he argues, is 'inconsistent with the convictions' the novelist held 'in general terms, of the fundamental inequalities between black and white'.[1] The problem, as has been implied, is of a different kind. It is one of making the story carry a meaning which, in this instance, is heavily loaded against any African upstart. Aladai (of *The African Witch*) whom Killam also describes as 'the creator trying to fashion a new ethic out of the old',[2] is, like Craven, a victim of the philosophical assumptions of the European imagination. What should be noted is not that they fail but that, though they are actually weak and inconsequential, they are seen by the European imagination as the light and hope of Africa. Their eventual failures therefore take on the character of doleful prophecy.

From this point of view, Gary's General Waitari is perhaps the most accomplished of these absurd heroes. Gary introduces him in a vein reminiscent of Mrs Aphra Behn's *Oroonoko*. For example, he struck the visiting American journalist 'at first glance with his extraordinary good looks which had an air of true nobility about them'. A 'black Caesar', as Gary writes, General Waitari wore his French cavalry officer's *képi* 'with the five stars of a full general on its sky-blue rim.'

> He was a Negro and his face was charcoal-black, and this gave his features, which were both delicate and of an almost classic hardness, a virile beauty which it was hard to forget. He was powerfully built, with shoulders, arms, and hands of an almost statuesque bearing, and he held his head back with an almost royal disdain (p. 280).

Waitari is not only a distinguished soldier, he is also an intellectual of some standing. His autobiography which he handed over to the journalist 'was profoundly French with its *lycées*, its scholarships all proudly set out, the Doctorat of Law, the books he had published, the various French

---

[1] See Killam, p. 75.   [2] Ibid., p. 153.

political groups and parties to which he had belonged, the Parliamentary Committees he had sat on—there was nothing missing' (p. 296). Waitari, then, was a kind of genius and the world seemed to expect great things from him. As the Negro writer, George Fenn, said of him: 'When Africa does raise its voice, this is the name that will be chiefly heard . . . unless the French make him their own Prime Minister' (p. 296). And again:

> There are several politicians of importance in Africa. There's N'krumah of Accra, Azikiwe of Nigeria, Awoluwa of the Jambas [sic], and Kenyatta of Kenya, now in prison. But there's also one of the most extraordinary men I have ever met, whether among white men or blacks: Waitari of French Equatorial Africa (p. 280).

Romain Gary casts Waitari in the role of chief antagonist to Morel and his mission in Chad. In this role, Waitari is a complex combination of African 'nationalist' and agent of French civilisation. In the one capacity, his task, as he explains it, is 'to rescue Africa from its savage past'. 'I can tell you that in our eyes factory chimneys are a thousand times more beautiful than the necks of giraffes, which our tourists admire so much. We are here to put an end to this sentimental nonsense about elephants and Africa, "the last Garden of Eden"' (p. 282). In his other role as the assimilated African, he is a worshipper of the culture of France. The American journalist, who had lived in Paris for several years, confessed that 'he had never heard anyone speak French with such talent and such power' (pp. 282–283). Indeed, Waitari had been carrying on a campaign 'for teaching French—and eliminating the African dialects' which he felt stood in the way of 'African' advancement (p. 283). French was therefore for him, 'the principal weapon of emancipation, unification and political education, the best way to carry out the fight against the primitive past'.

> The Oulé dialect contained no word for 'nation', no word for 'country', no word for 'politics', no words for 'worker,' 'working-class,' 'proletariat'; 'Marxism,' or 'socialism' were quite beyond

C

its vocabulary, and indeed the expression 'the right of peoples to self-determination' became 'victory of the Oulés over their enemies' (p. 283).

But predictably enough, the two roles can only lead to frustration and absurdity, and this marvel of Africa faces a doom similar to that of other *evolué*-heroes of the European novel of Africa. 'However this great man's ambition,' the journalist thought before leaving him, 'his loneliness was even greater. . . . It is always pathetic to watch the efforts a man makes to cling to a straw, especially when one is one-self the straw. And so his eyes followed him with a certain sympathy and no little sadness' (p. 314).

Obviously, then, the European novel of Africa invariably raises the same general issues and resolves them in almost the same predictable manner. The terms of argument in these novels are virtually fixed; the arguments they advance, however refined and subtle they may seem, are fully qualified and often totally dependent on the many traditions of European intellectual and cultural history. Only indirectly, as it were by accident, are these novels about Africa in any important sense.

It is against this background that Cary's four novels of Africa will be examined and evaluated. In fact, only against it can the fascinating intellectual and critical problems raised by them be profitably understood. Obviously, Cary's novels, like the other foreign novels of Africa, will reflect the moods and eras of European intellectual and moral history. For that reason, at least, genuine correlations can and ought to be established wherever possible between the handling of the theme of Africa in these novels and the changing attitudes in European fiction to other issues, the working classes, for example. Following such a correlation, the reader may begin to see what is so true of the novels: that they represent the response of a particular European mind at a particular moment in time to the peoples and the phenomena of Africa. To be able to do this satisfactorily, one should also try to define the particular artistic forms which this particular mind uses to communicate his prejudices and meanings and to see where and how he differs, ultimately, from the many others who preceded him in that attempt. There can be no doubt, everything considered, that Cary deserves this effort in criticism. What requires doing is to place that achievement in context through a critical (and discriminating) examination of the individual novels.

2: *Pagan and Christian*

Though *Aissa Saved* definitely anticipates the theme of religious conflict which Cary was to develop at length in *The African Witch*,[1] it did not begin with Aissa and religion but with Ali and education. In the Preface to *Aissa Saved*, Cary makes it clear that he wanted to study the effect of education on a 'rather shy and not very clever boy' Ali. 'I was anxious to contrast Ali's standards and ideas with those about him. This, of course, involved questions of local ethics, local religion, the whole conflict of those ideas in a primitive community; and also the impact of new ideas from outside.'[2] The theme of religion, however, became an overriding one. 'Ethics are important enough, goodness knows, but the fundamental question for everybody is what they live by; what is their faith' (p. 8).

To answer that question, Cary began to establish and develop the character of Aissa as it is shaped by her 'faith'. In the process, as Cary himself points out, Aissa 'gradually became the heroine *because she was more central to a deeper* interest, that of religion' (p. 8; italics added). That interest led Cary to a specific question about Aissa's faith: 'how will it stand the big knock; how deep does it send its roots into reality?' Cary's answer in the Preface is unequivocal: 'Faith in ju-ju' cannot stand the 'big knock': 'a few dry years, a

---

[1] Charles G. Hoffmann, 'Joyce Cary's African Novels: "There's a War on"', *South Atlantic Quarterly*, LXII (Spring, 1963), p. 282, points out that *Aissa Saved* 'contains the seminal ideas and explores the themes which are to become the central focus of the succeeding African novels'.

[2] 'Prefatory Essay' to *Aissa Saved*, Carfax ed. (London; 1952), pp. 7–8. Subsequent references are to this edition and will be cited in parentheses.

very little "contamination" from a government instructor destroys faith in a lingam' (p. 8).

In the novel itself, however, Cary somehow refuses to press this conclusion. Rather he examines two related issues. One is the tenacity with which ignorance and faith can combine to perpetuate basically irrational and often cruel religions. This tenacity is symbolised in Moshalo. The other issue, of which Aissa is the symbol, is the ease with which such ignorance and faith can be carried over from one religion into another. For the purposes of Cary's intellectual argument in *Aissa Saved*, this second issue was the crucial one. Yet in order to represent it adequately and to supply the background of religious fatalism with which Aissa's Christianity is eventually 'adulterated', Cary had also to develop the first of these issues. He had to establish the logic of feeling by which Moshalo and Aissa could accept their ju-ju-worship and Christianity and find fulfilment in them. This, in effect, meant an account of the emotional and personal roots of Aissa's and Moshalo's faith. 'All those in fact, who do not cut their throats and many who do, have some kind of faith; if only in a political theory, "science", a mascot or a column of mud roughly shaped like an erect penis' (p. 8).

The consideration of these two issues does not always lead to a unified statement or insight. For example, if one assumes, as Cary does, that Moshalo's faith cannot stand the 'big knock', then it would be virtually impossible to present it as having any intrinsic or lasting usefulness. If, in addition, one assumes that the Christian missions brought to Africa 'a far better faith than any native construction', as Cary's Preface claims, then the novel can only show the disastrous effects of the interaction of Christianity and paganism within the African mind. In effect, the fanaticism of the convert is not explained in terms of the inherent weakness of all religions, and the individual African convert rather than Religion itself becomes the victim of the conversion-process. 'I think, from experience,' Cary states in the Preface, 'that some Christian missions do not realise the effect of telling African primitives that God is "Almighty!", or "Omnipotent" and allowing them, uncorrected, to suppose that this means not "the final power in the universe" but the "one who can do all things." So they blame God for a sore throat, and thank him for a fine day or a good bargain' (pp. 8–9).

It becomes clear immediately that Cary cannot deal with the transference of faith from one 'religion' to another without in the process subverting this absolute contrast which his Preface tries to establish between the pagan and the Christian imaginations. Because Cary is seriously enough committed to his two intuitions—the tenacity of primitive religious experience, and the tragic absurdity of a collation of that experience with Christianity—he tries hard to do justice to both religions.[1] But because neither intuition can be affirmed absolutely without loss to the other, there develops an inevitable uncertainty in the novel as to the final significance of Aissa's career, and as to the spirit in which, in the final analysis, the novel's title should be taken.

One explanation for this is to be found in Cary's handling of the theme of sacrifice as a means of atonement. First, Cary places the urge among the pagans to offer sacrifice alongside the Christian doctrine preached by the Carrs of redemption based on Christ's willing self-sacrifice. Secondly (and this follows from the first), he suggests that this sacrificial element in Christianity appealed so strongly to Aissa and the others precisely because it spoke directly to their own concept of religion, to that worship of blood allegedly already deeply rooted in juju. Ojo thus appropriately devotes many of his sermons to accounts of Christ's physical suffering for the redemption of man.

[1] Compare this with the parallel difficulty Kant had in trying to draw down God into relations with men, to make Him a principle working in and upon them after he had established that God could logically only be a transcendent being, isolated from all other beings even though He is their Author and Maintainer. See Edward Caird, *The Critical Philosophy of Kant* (Glasgow, 1909), pp. 523–524, for a discussion of this aspect of Kant's *Religion within the Bounds of Mere Reason*.

30

This need for sacrifice, deriving in part from the holy precedent of Christ's own willing self-sacrifice, dominates the life of the converts in the novel. The hymns they sing return to this theme and celebrate the gory as well as the magical details of Christ's death. When Aissa sang the verses,

> All things I like best
> I sacrifice to His blood,

she 'rolled her head and eyes in almost mournful fashion [and] raised her flat nose to the sky' (p. 49). Intoxicated by their zeal and faith, they believe the blood of Christ will save them from death and bullets.

> Brimah, the carrier, a man known for his good sense, smiled and said: 'What about the police?' meaning the government police, armed with carbines, 'Suppose they shoot.'
> But Nagulo laughed at him. 'They can't hurt us after we drink Jesus' blood.'
> 'Can't they? Have you tried?'
> Shangoedi flew at him: 'You fool, did Jesus die, could they kill him? Jesus' blood cannot die' (pp. 132–133).

The impulse to sacrifice reaches its most crucial demonstration in Aissa's sacrifice of her only son, Abba. Taking the baby from her back and putting it into Bayu's arms, she says in English, 'Take him and throw him in da fire. He's no good. I no lak him no more' (p. 203).

> With trembling hands she took off its cloth and wrapped it round a stone which she held to her heart while she hurried to the river, She wept loudly: 'Oh Jesus, you right, I love him better, oh dear, me poor lil baby, oh, I doan want to give him up. Oh baby, don cry no mo. You go to Heaven, Jesus make you happy for Heaven.'
> Then she threw the stone into the river and flung herself down uttering loud howls: 'Oh my poo lil baby, Oh Jesus, I give you all. You go way now' (p. 204).

Aissa's child was born a witch, 'a sickly little creature with a large umbilical hernia'. Aissa was 'advised' by the local people to put it out of the way. 'But Aissa, in spite of advice and threats, would not give up the child' (p. 46). Abba is saved from early death by Ojo who rescues Aissa from a mob and brings her and her child to the mission. Aissa never forgets this. She 'had never ceased to be grateful to Jesus who had saved her from misery and her baby from the witch-finders, and she always sought to please him' (p. 48). Aissa's sacrifice of her son for Christ's sake is, in this context, her supreme Christian gesture, her attempt to assert her love for Christ by giving to him 'all things I like best'.

It is nevertheless quite evident that Aissa is acting towards Jesus as she would have acted towards Oke, that not her gods, but the titles of her gods, had changed. This view is reinforced by the parallel single-mindedness with which the ju-ju-worshippers in the novel also demand and expect sacrifice to please or appease their gods, the closest example being Ishe's unwilling surrender of her son, Numi, to Oke.

> Owule brought beer and she drank it thirstily like water. The sweat was pouring from her. Her legs failed and she tumbled down. The drummers came round her and beat over her body, which writhed and jerked to the music. She jumped up and ran about screaming (p. 123).

As Miss Mahood and other critics have pointed out, the ju-ju-worshippers and the converts are not alone in placing so much value on sacrifice. Mrs Carr lost her two babies because of a deliberate refusal to interrupt her missionary work in order to serve her health. Her husband realised that, like the converts, she was intent on martyrdom.

> 'My dear Hilda, do be reasonable. . . .
> You don't want to get us killed.'
> 'We're not going to get killed, and if we are, it doesn't make any difference. We might die any day of something' (pp. 52–53).

Mrs Carr's grounds for risking death are as irrational as the converts'. 'Aissa's bad conduct, her ingratitude so unexpected, enraged her like a piece of treachery aimed at the heart of her faith, and she was quite ready to be martyred on the spot as a kind of protest against it or, as some might put it, in revenge' (p. 53). Indeed her very presence in Africa as a missionary's wife was a protest against life: 'lame, sick, tortured by worry and anxiety', she found that the African adventure 'offered itself like an escape. She flew to it like a clerk to war or a ruined man to drink. But it was no good explaining this to her because she had no brain to understand it and had a complete answer to all criticism. What she felt to be right was God's will' (p. 25).

The degree of Carr's affinity with the primitive religious imagination of Hilda and Aissa is obscured by the responsibilities which he felt he owed to social and political order. He believed in God and the Devil; accordingly, whenever he felt a serious set-back, when 'luck was against him' he felt his enemy as 'a personal force, as the Devil himself, penetrating all existence, as manifold and plastic as life itself, but much more cunning. He could feel him in the immense darkness which surrounded him, like a watchful breathing soul' (p. 25). But beneath his awareness that he could only propagate his faith in that district '*dum bene se gesserit*', there was an inevitable urge in him to help assert the Divine Will. He could wonder how 'to defeat a power which was capable of using such as Ojo and Hilda for his own ends' (p. 25). When he meets the converts as they canoed to the village singing a favourite Christian hymn, he is duly overcome. The converts 'stared anxiously at him' and 'saw to their surprise that he, too, and Mrs Carr, were singing with them'. The sight of 'their master's enthusiasm as he beat time vigorously with Hilda's hand tightly grasped in his, removed all their doubts. Every voice joined in, and loud cries urged the paddlers to go on' (p. 28). With 'gratitude for her love and sympathy, for all God's goodness and the power of His spirit, he joined with her in the crowning verse . . . "Grant me now my soul's desire, None of self and all of thee"'. (p. 29).

Cary claimed in one of his letters that the novel was a study of 'the effect of several kinds of education, atheist in Bradgate and Ali, materialist in Jacob, Christianity in the Carrs and Aissa, pagan in others, Mohammedan in the Emir'.[1] Cary, it would seem, was opposed to the self-abandonment

[1] Quoted by Hoffmann, op. cit., *South Atlantic Quarterly*, LXII (Spring, 1963), pp. 230.

involved in both Christianity and paganism and sought to substitute a faith which would eliminate both sacrifice and self-sacrifice. In the event, Cary was able to present Aissa's faith not only as a perversion of Christianity but also as a too-literal acceptance of it. Either way, it was a dangerous faith because it put enthusiasm in place of reason and chose sacrifice instead of regeneration. As Cary wrote to Ernest Benn, his publisher, the novel was 'in one sense an attack on one kind of sacrifice. It seeks to show that the idea of sacrifice when removed from that of utility, of service, i.e. pleasing God, pleasing Oke, becomes pure ju-ju and also self-indulgence.'[1] In his Notebooks, Cary reiterates this point: 'Self-sacrifice as an ideal (for its own sake) is moral defeatism or sensual indulgence. It is probably pathological either in origin or manifestation, and belongs to all primitive religion.'[2]

There is a third side to the argument of the novel brought to focus by the long spell of dry weather which is the immediate occasion for the most violent religious conflict in Yanrin. The Christians and the pagans pray to their respective gods for rain in order thereby to establish the superiority of their own faith. Bradgate and Ali, the rationalists, know that prayers, whether Christian or pagan, will not bring rain. But when the rain does fall, after the 'fall' of Owule, the priestess, and the sacrifice of Numi to Oke, both the Christians and the pagans claim the credit (p. 125). We have already noted Cary's criticism of the religious enthusiasm of the Carrs and the pagans. Cary was against Bradgate and Ali, not because they did not believe in miracles, but because they seemed unaware of the potency of the primitive religious ardour supporting faith. Douglas Stewart has argued that 'missionaries accustomed to the secular agnosticism of Europe are singularly ill-equipped to grapple with the seething, imaginatively religious life of less sophisticated people.[3] Cary

[1] Quoted in M. M. Mahood, *Joyce Cary's Africa* (London, 1964), p. 119.

[2] Quoted in Mahood, p. 116.

[3] Douglas Stewart, *The Ark of God*, London, 1961, pp. 140–141.

would have added that the Carrs, as representatives of Christianity, were as far from the secular agnosticism of Europe as Aissa and Moshalo. Stewart is right, however, when he claims that 'it is not faith these Africans lack, but scepticism'.[1] It is a misunderstanding of Cary's purpose, therefore, to complain of 'an essential aloofness' on his part, 'from the tensions and issues that go forward'.[2] Cary is deeply involved in the issues at stake and does pass his judgement—which is against all three camps. The complications of actual life (the constants of life) simply do not allow for the simplistic solutions offered by believers in Christ, Oke or Science. That these believers mean well is nothing against Cary's argument.

It is worth noting, however, that the argument of *Aissa Saved* does not always succeed in moving away from the limitations of its African context towards a general statement on the nature of the religious imagination anywhere. It is true that Cary's characterisation of Aissa suggests this universality of religious feeling. This is especially so in the scene at the end of the novel when Aissa's death seems justified by the mystical experience of her son's resurrection.

> Immediately the sky was rolled up like a door curtain and she saw before her the great hall of God with pillars of mud painted white and red. God, in a white riga and a new indigo turban, his hands heavy with thick silver rings, stood in the middle and beside him the spirit like a goat with white horns. Abba was sitting on its back looking frightened and almost ready to cry. One of the angels was holding him and putting his cap straight. The others were laughing at him and clapping their hands (p. 211).

This vivid (and local) definition of Aissa's apocalyptic vision is clearly a *Christian* 'triumph', and may be contrasted with the situation at the end of *The African Witch* where pagan Elizabeth and her religion of blood win. In that novel the victory is meant to represent that of Africa over Europe, of ju-ju over Christianity, of passion over intellect. Nevertheless,

[1] Ibid., p. 141.
[2] Bloom, *The Indeterminate World*, p. 47.

even in *Aissa Saved*, this triumph is not a final or con-
clusive victory of one system over another, but of one
believer over another believer, of Aissa and Ojo over Moshalo
and Owule. It is Aissa, not Christianity, that triumphs over
Moshalo; not Oke, the ju-ju, is defeated but its worshippers. It
is part of Cary's meaning in the novel to make the distinction
between the religious expression and the religious imagination, between the integrity of Aissa's faith and the limitations
of that faith as a system of life. In this sense, then, we can
believe in the authenticity of Aissa's apocalyptic vision
because we accept the simple integrity of her religious imagination.

Yet there is an overall problem of interpretation which
derives from a kind of dichotomy in the novel's view of itself
and its audience. In its simplest form, this dichotomy is
found in the hints Cary gives of the audience he is addressing
in the novel. 'The rival parties [in Yanrin],' Cary writes in
the novel, 'were quite as angry and obstinate *as those of a
Sunday School at home debating the place and time of the annual
treat*' (p. 17; italics added). 'At home' looks back to England
(or Ireland) and to the English audience of the novel. The
very existence of this special audience implies, inevitably, a
particular bias in presentation and argument; it assumes
everything which the audience can be expected to bring with
it in the reading of the novel. Cary's role thus becomes that
of an interpreter of an alien culture, who is naturally obliged
(and inclined) to insist on certain dramatic contrasts between
the European and the African situations in his narrative.
Hence, in spite of every other consideration, Aissa's vision
of the Holy *Ghost* is that of a holy '*goat* with white horns'.
Hence also the triumphant converts wear 'a page of the
Bible slung from their necks' and believe themselves safe
against the police carbines (p. 183). Hence, finally, there is
no African character in the novel who escapes the frantic and
agonised life of either the Christians or the pagans, or even
accepts them with what may be called a normal human
excitement.

It is hardly surprising, therefore, that the novel's major concern, the study of the religious imagination, assumes the character of a revelation of a local 'African mentality'. Scene after scene depicts the unthinking, childlike stupidity of the converts, their wild, almost animal delight in clearly purposeless action, their fervent devotion to the white masters and their complete incapacity for sustained concentration of either mind or body to any task in hand. Conveniently, too, the characters are so chosen that they are necessarily incapable of either thought or circumspection, and in particular, are saved from all adult responsibility either to themselves or to their community. There is, inevitably, a pathetically ludicrous dimension to this presentation which runs contrary to the high seriousness which is supposed to pervade their action in the novel. It is not surprising, also, that some critics should read the novel as a revelation and draw wider conclusions from it about the effects of Christianity on the African.[1]

One such African is Ojo, presented as good and dutiful but clearly dedicated to a cause which he obviously cannot fully define or even understand. His background had nothing of value in it: he was, in fact, one of the 'kind turned out every year in large quantities by the new civilisation on the Coast'. Since his conversion he had become 'the most faithful and devoted' pupil and protégé the Carrs had. Now turned preacher and organiser for the new faith, he proves, as the novel says, that his 'love for Jesus' is 'sincere and lasting' (p. 16). Yet Cary represents Ojo's revivalist faith quite differently from his presentation of other religious enthusiasts in his European novels. In *To Be a Pilgrim*, for instance, Wilcher was filled with 'horror' at the thought of his sister Lucy in the arms of the revivalist preacher, Brown: 'In that horror,' Wilcher admitted, 'was my understanding. The

---

[1] Walter Allen, *Joyce Cary* (London, 1954), p. 10; Charles G. Hoffmann, op. cit., p. 232, Andrew Wright, *Joyce Cary: A Preface to His Novels* (London, 1958), p. 59 and Jack Wolkenfeld, *Joyce Cary: The Developing Style* (New York, 1968), ch. 1.

words came into my mind, "And she shall be offered for a sacrifice"'.[1]

Brown was the perfect symbol of that kind of religion which Wilcher detested and feared, a religion 'which appealed only to the feelings and the nerves'. Lucy, his sister, felt otherwise. As Wilcher was to find out, Lucy and the other followers would often exclaim 'in their quiet voices, Hallelujah, or Amen', as Brown spoke. 'I saw Lucy utter such an ejaculation,' Wilcher confessed, 'and it gave me a sense of horror and disgust'.[2] But Wilcher's disgust, though justified by the actual violence of Brown's religion, soon yields to understanding, even respect. 'The swelling voices, the sight of these people, let out I suppose for a dinner hour and still in their working clothes, again made tremble in me that nerve which always responded to the ancient call of the apostles, "Leave all and follow Christ".' Wilcher's understanding of and respect for this primitive ('ancient') religious feeling is induced by the dedication of its adherents rather than by the form of its faith. Ella, for example, whose humiliation had filled Wilcher 'with something more than disgust' knelt to Brown's prayers, 'with her hands pressed together, her face, stained with tears, turned up with an expression of such humility and adoration that my knees faltered beneath me'.[3] The argument of *Aissa Saved* never comes so far as to suggest in a positive way that the religion of feeling which Ojo adopts is of this same kind. The novel, that is, does not see Ojo's faith as similar to Brown's—a response to the 'ancient call' of the apostles. For faith, in such circumstances, is a Cause: 'A cause. Excitement, the experience of suffering, of humiliation, so attractive to my sense. Above all, an answer to everything.'[4]

Aissa Saved is essentially a study of the religious imagination in action and specifically within the context of Africa and among Africans. In this sense, as we have implied, it is also a novel of Africa, a foreign novel. Miss Mahood warns her

[1] *To Be A Pilgrim*, Carfax ed. (London, 1951), pp. 59–60.
[2] Ibid., p. 60.   [3] Ibid., p. 66.   [4] Ibid., p. 69.

readers, quite rightly, that 'an acquaintance with the [original] scene itself, a sight of the sketches and a study of the work in all its stages must not lead us into thinking that Cary set about writing novels of Nigerian life in exactly the way Constable set about painting Dedham Vale'.[1] Accordingly, she argues that the scene (pp. 153–154) of Aissa's possession during her first communion derives from 'a sequence of self-abandonment, possession by evil spirits, exorcism of the evil spirits and possession by a good spirit', which 'found expression in many religions and, Cary believed, has distorted the best of them'.[2] Aissa, that is, could have been English or French.

This, clearly, is not the whole argument of *Aissa Saved* because, in common with most serious foreign fiction, one of its problems is to determine what to attribute to character— the personality of an independent human spirit in a context of action—and what to environment and race. *Aissa Saved* does speak of the universality of the religious imagination and does depend, ultimately, on an empiricist's definition of human psychology. In that sense, Aissa's responses can be given a validity on the basis of what we may call the general laws of human nature. Aissa is, nevertheless, presented specifically as the product of an African environment. Her responses, natural as they might be, cannot be separated from what must, in the context of the novel, be regarded as her 'native' instincts and habits of mind. Her thought processes are assumed to be (and are presented as) different in some essential ways from those of the Carrs, Bradgate and the novel's primary audience. In presenting her, therefore, the novelist is necessarily 'revealing' her kind to the audience. For it is one of the characteristics of the foreign novel that it tries (and its readers hope) to derive conclusions that would apply not only to the characters as individuals but also to the entire continent and its people. It seeks to describe an experience which it knows is unusual to its primary audience in a

[1] M. M. Mahood, op. cit., p. vii.
[2] Ibid; p. 109.

39

manner which will keep it suitably and permanently unusual in spite of the new familiarity.

This is a problem some of the implications of which have been mentioned earlier. It is mentioned again in order to emphasise that *Aissa Saved*, like any other foreign novels of Africa, cannot help being about Africa; that, in particular, *Aissa Saved* is urged on to some of its very general conclusions by the attraction of an environmental determinism. The theme of a war of faiths which Cary claimed to be central to the novel is accordingly surrounded by a rival theme of Africa. It is true, as Miss Mahood has also argued, that Cary used Borgu and Kontagora 'as a satisfyingly distanced setting for a book about the fundamental injustice of the world and the varying faiths by which individuals come to their own terms with this injustice.'[1] This, 'rather than the parallel savageries of ju-ju and debased Christianity' is the novel's main theme. 'Once we have seized the book's theme we are likely to complain that it has too much form rather than too little. . . . Our discomfort in reading it comes less from any horrors of the story than from the unrelenting thematic use to which much of the story is put.'[2] It is nevertheless true that the 'horrors' of *Aissa Saved* contribute as much to the theme of 'fundamental injustice' as they do to the rival theme of Africa which, in the Preface to *The African Witch*, Cary claims needed a violence of narrative to keep the story in its place. The violence of *Aissa Saved*, in that light, is a necessary way, from a European point of view, of doing justice to the fact as well as the feeling of Africa. It represents a turmoil of spirit externalised in the frenzy and emotionalism of the novel's African characters.

Aissa Saved, then, qualified but did not abandon the theme of Africa. The devoted Christian revivalists of *Except the Lord* had as 'mistaken' a notion of Christianity as the converts of *Aissa Saved*. Believing literally (as did St Paul) in a Second Coming 'calculated in London for April 15, 1868', they had loyally assembled to greet the occasion. 'It was

[1] M. M. Mahood, op. cit., p. 106.   [2] Ibid., p. 106.

40

faith that made me submissive', Nimmo confessed. 'Those who deride our folly and credulity might ask why the poor mother among her hunger-wasted children should not believe that if Christ truly loved the poor and the outcasts He would come again to rescue them from misery.'[1] *Except the Lord* goes on to 'understand' the rationale behind this obviously superstitious ('primitive') religious feeling and to make a case against all rationalism.

> The marvel is that millions deny all hope and boast themselves as men who for some reason of fear or vanity take care to ask no questions that cannot be answered with a slide rule, who learn nothing, state nothing, but numbers, who, carefully withdrawing their dignity from the arena where men struggle and suffer so foolishly, take their padded seats in the stalls and raise critical eyebrows at the circus which is the agony of the world.[2]

Without pleading for general superstitiousness, Cary can state the context of its power, the dimensions of the kind of order which it brings.

In *Aissa Saved*, the expectation of rain through the mediation of Christian prayer or pagan sacrifice is not seen as parallel to the expectation of Christ's coming. The roots of that expectation in the personality and personal needs of the characters are not determined. In other words, what (for Cary) would have been the ultimate justification for such irrationality is not similarly explored. In fact, Cary's tone is ironically casual and seems intended to undermine the seriousness with which the converts take their faith:

> The Christians promised that rain would fall within an hour. Ojo explained to God, as he had heard Mr. Carr explain and as far as possible in the same words, the needs of his people, and asked him to forgive them in their sins, to take pity upon them in their extremity, and send a good rain.
>
> All the Christians prayed, beating their heads on the ground. Those who did not know what Ojo was saying and knew no other formula repeated in English: 'Jesus loves me', and added in their own tongue: 'Hear us, God, hear us. We fear too much. . . . It

[1] *Except the Lord* (New York, 1962), pp. 109, 110, 112.
[2] Ibid., p. 113.

small ting for you to make rain fall. Oh God, you open your heart—you hear us—you our fadder and mudder' (p. 196).

Put beside this the account of the final minutes of the abortive expectation of the Second Coming in *Except the Lord*. As 'colour crept up into the light,' the congregation sang Wesley's hymn, welcoming the Coming of the Lord:

> Once for favour'd sinners slain
> Thousand and thousand saints attending
> Swell the triumph of his train
> Alleluia
> Christ appears on earth again.

But the 'light' is only an illusion:

> The minister had started again to pray, but even I, as I knelt there, knew that what stood before us was not the end of the world but a fine sunrise not uncommon at that season on the high moon. Within a few minutes the sun itself appeared upon the edge of the moon like a row of sparks on a half-drenched brand. The sword-like rays faded from the air and the clouds turned from ruby, amethyst and opal to pale gold.
>
> I do not know how long we knelt and how long the minister prayed. It was my father who first rose from his knees and lifted us to our feet.[1]

The possibility of comedy in this passage is firmly excluded by the integrity of the narrator's heart, and the tradition of the Psalms which he invokes: 'I will lift up mine eyes unto the hills from whence come my help.'[2] It is excluded also by Nimmo's earlier denial of the view that 'only the most stupid and illiterate persons adhered to that sect. This is not so'.[3] It is excluded, finally, by the underlying vision of the novel that 'those who choose the mountain tops for that intuition of the numinous in us, in which it seems that we break through the boundaries of the world into the very centre of the Divine Mind, are not deceived'.[4] What is most lacking in *Aissa Saved*, which by its very nature as a foreign

---

[1] *Except the Lord* (New York, 1962), pp. 115–116.
[2] Ibid., p. 114.   [3] Ibid., p. 112.   [4] Ibid., p. 114.

novel it cannot always avoid lacking, is the explicit endorsement of what in *Except the Lord* Cary calls 'the mighty and everlasting pressure of the soul seeking by ways unseen, and often unsuspected, its own good, freedom and enlightenment'.[1]

[1] Ibid., p. 150.

3: Order and Civilisation

An American Visitor is almost explicitly a study in the nature of order and civilisation. As is typical of Cary in his best work, the approach to the question is oblique and his conclusions superficially only tentative. Yet the complication of human, political and intellectual situations in the novel does enforce a most definitely humane argument relevant not only to the immediate African world of the novel, but to all civilisations and all epochs.

In its external action, the novel is about Birri and its untidy internal social and political problems complicated by the presence of English tin prospectors armed with mining permits issued in London. An American anthropologist has also arrived in the area. Reputed among both the Europeans and the Africans as a 'loose' woman, she is officially in Birri to report on the local culture. In the course of this, however, she undertakes to propagate her anarchical ideas of self-determination and anti-imperialism among the Birri. The local British Resident, Mr. Bewsher, caught between conflicting interests, is unable to avert the threatening upheaval. On the one side are the cold official instructions he receives from his superiors and the pressures put on him by the business-minded prospectors. On the other side is his temperament which inclines him to seek to promote what he considers the genuine long-term interests of the local people. His difficulty is in being both British bureaucrat and pagan man at once, in having to 'take responsibility for dodging [his] own laws or breaking [his] own rebels', as Cary says of political officers in the Preface to the novel.[1]

[1] Prefatory Essay to *An American Visitor*, Carfax ed., (London, 1952), p. 11. Subsequent references are to this edition and will be cited in parentheses at the end of quotations.

Beneath this apparently political or administrative problem is an intellectual question which *An American Visitor* also examines. British colonial rule in the 1920s and '30s was based for the most part on what has been called the system of Indirect Rule. This policy accepted the necessity for imperial power but held that Britain had the responsibility for preserving and even developing those local institutions which the local governors found deserving. In practice, it was easy enough to meet the need for imperial presence and power. The other responsibility, it was found, involved delicate decisions as to the value of local political, cultural and even religious institutions and practices. In addition, opinion was divided among the governors and administrators some of whom contended that ALL 'native' institutions should be preserved and that NO European values should be imposed. Their reasoning took many forms: that European 'civilisation' would be a corrupting influence on the African, or that the African was not mentally equipped to benefit from change and 'progress'.[1] The presence and character of Miss Hasluck in *An American Visitor* provide the occasion and the vehicle for a full consideration of the entire question of civilisation and primitivism and of the proper responsibilities of imperial rule in the circumstances of Africa.

Primarily, however, Cary works towards his study through people, black and white, high and low, especially through the itinerant single girl who gives the novel its title. Marie Hasluck, journalist, anthropologist, American, has no other God but the man she has come to love. Her development in the novel is firmly set out, although Cary makes her growth

[1] Jim Latter of Joyce Cary's novel of the post-1918 English politics, *Not Honour More*, felt quite strongly that colonial peoples should be left in their blessed poverty in order that the integrity of European rule and civilisation may be vindicated. His book, *The Lugas and British African Policy: The Great Betrayal* which he refers to in *Not Honour More* was devoted to stating this position at length: 'I wrote this book ten years ago when I was hounded out of the African service for trying to protect my people, the Lugas, from the government policy of what they call civilisation but is really materialism and general European degeneracy.'

45

mysterious by making her uncertain of the power behind her own changing and maturing attitudes to Africa, to the imperial question and to men.

> . . . the quality of life had nothing to do with any special kind of lawfulness or dress or religion. Two Birri men arm in arm might be much better off than the most civilised kind of people, who had been brought up in mutual distrust and watchfulness and jealousy instead of sympathy. And their happiness was more secure (p. 115).

Quietly, her thought moves from the security of this happiness among the Birri—this life which was 'valid' in itself without respect to specific laws, costumes or religion—to her own life and happinesss with Bewsher:

> . . . this new kind of experience in which she moved awkwardly and doubtfully like a child at her first party was not a holiday, an escape from daily endurances [as her earlier affairs had been], but life itself. It could not come to an end because it was natural and real, the right kind of living. To love and be loved (pp. 115–116).

By making her define 'the good life' in a moment of half-conscious reverie, Cary makes her statement more genuine. At the same time, he makes her momentarily unconscious of the larger significance of her position. In that frame of mind, in the happiness of her new experience, even the 'piece of broken ground', 'the washed-down ruins' of huts, the 'grey moon, the grey fields, the smoke grey wall of the forest behind the falling sheets of dusty light'—all of them brought to her 'without any thought of them . . . the mysterious physical excitement which acknowledges a grand beauty. Her being felt it [and the mystic and sexual symbolism of Lawrence's *The Rainbow* and Hardy's *Jude the Obscure* are surely both recalled here] as the dreamer acknowledges the cathedral overhead by a quickened sense of man's privilege and God's eternity.'

> It was real, this life . . . it was more real than any other kind of life because now when she looked out from it, from this secure delight and trust, all things fell with their harmonies, the flesh was reconciled with the spirit, the mind with the heart, egotism with sacrifice, self with other self. When she took Bewsher in her arms she did not

give or take, she entered into a completeness without limits or division, without description or laws. It was the life of life, the centre of being (p. 116).

As she understands Bewsher better, she comes to appreciate the kind of attitude to the responsibilities and the complexities of social and political life of Africa which distinguishes him from his colleagues and superiors. She was originally afraid of Bewsher's 'optimism'. of his assurance that 'everything would happen just as he wished it to happen' (pp. 121–122). She now sees that this optimism was his only way out of the cynicism of Alabaster or the romanticism of those who took unnecessary risks in order to attain 'any kind of dramatic apotheosis' (p. 121). As Marie kneels by Bewsher's grave at the end of the novel, she feels an absurdity in her worship of him. 'She looked up and apologised [to Gore and Cottee]. "I'm not praying, but where Monkey [Bewsher] is, the ground feels kind of different"' (p. 239).

The human or personal situation in *An American Visitor* is not restricted to Marie Hasluck's romance with Bewsher. Bewsher himself is not only shown as the stiff administrator, but as an incorrigible rascal. Hence Cottee respects him but also understands that there is 'a good deal of hokum' about the man (p. 239). It was thus possible for Cary to portray Bewsher as a dedicated 'pagan-man' without having to make him a solemn hero. Bewsher would thus have become the deserving representative of civilisation, one of 'that devoted corps of hard-working officials' who, according to Harold R. Collins, 'for all their occasional bungling, try manfully to be pillars of decency, order and progressive authority in the British African dependencies'.[1] Cary's method is to understate his worth. Hence, during the heated debate between Marie and Cottee on the quality of Birri civilisation, Bewsher's comments (which are most sensible in the circumstances) are yet offered with the casualness of irresponsible repartee.

[1] Harold R. Collins, 'Joyce Cary's Troublesome Africans', *Antioch Review*, XX (Fall, 1953), p. 406.

> Bewsher, who was sitting between them smoking a large curly pipe and admiring the fire, remarked that in fact there was very little crime in Birri. Marie at once appealed to him. 'Mr Bewsher, you agree with me that Birri is run by traditional custom—it *is* a system of natural rights and obligations——'
>
> Bewsher took his pipe out of his mouth and looked enquiringly at the excited young woman. 'Natural?' and then after a pause, 'You mean family feeling—that sort of thing' . . .
>
> 'I mean the whole system—the co-operative idea of it.'
>
> Bewsher said that he was afraid Birri didn't run itself if that was what she meant. It had to be kept to the mark (p. 90).

The local people are also shown responding in a personal way to the pressures of their changing material and spiritual condition. The chiefs lament the collapse of their authority and the end of 'all decency and good behaviour'. Faced with the threat by the younger men to attack the British station,

> Old white-headed men, meeting night after night, not at the judgment tree but in some secluded hut where none of the youngsters would look for them, uttered groans of distress.
>
> 'What next—we'll all be destroyed' (p. 156).

From these complications of issues and situations Cary could have avoided the censure of his critics by writing a novel which would offer a dogmatic solution to the problems of politics, culture and civilisation. Cary chose rather to explore the issues involved in the context of the human reality he knew very well. He sought to express those truths about these issues which would depend, ultimately, on the world of actual men while at the same time appealing to their 'conceptual feelings'. In other words, he aspired to the ideal of the novelist so clearly defined in *Art and Reality*:

> The novelist must show his meaning by creating persons who have the character of actual persons, in a world that could be actual but displays a moral order that does not present itself in life. It is an ideal order which remains an object of attainment for that writer in the world as he knows it in fact.[1]

When the novel was published in 1933, it gained as well as

[1] *Art and Reality* (New York, 1961), p. 179.

suffered from the topicality of its subject. While the novel was studying anarchism and self-determination in Marie Hasluck, the newspapers and the public were already debating the same subject in relation to world politics. The second Conference of the Communist International had followed Lenin and the general drift of the post-war European thought in asking for self-determination for dependent peoples, and for the liquidation of Imperial possessions. The League of Nations, a non-Imperial international force, was also in jeopardy. 'Fascist States', the *New Statesman and Nation* declared, 'are by their nature anarchistic.' Germany, Japan and Italy were opposed to the League, the paper argued, because such an international body would put a 'check on [their] imperialistic and militarist ambitions' and so come into conflict with the idea of 'the sovereignty of the state' as the 'sacred and final institution whose expansion and power [justified] every aggression'.[1]

While Cottee, in *An American Visitor*, lamented the loss of the Empire 'simply because we don't know how to keep it together. Just encouraging people everywhere to be rebels' (p. 97), the students at Oxford, no longer impressed by Rhodes' claim that the English were 'the first race in the world', and that 'the more of the world we inherit the better it is for the human race',[2] were passing their momentous resolution that they 'will in no circumstances fight for King and country'.[3] In the novel, the exasperated Stoker, leaning 'once more over the cartridges' wondered where 'these politicals' got their 'pacifism' from. 'Is it Oxford, or where?'

> 'Just a fashion,' said Dollar. 'It came in about the time the top-hat went out. I believe Lugard started it out here. Any rate these lads all copy it as soon as they arrive. It's just like school all over again' (p. 181).

[1] 'Back to Anarchy', *New Statesman and Nation*, 16 December 1933, p. 800.
[2] Quoted by Dorothy Crisp, 'For King and Country', *Saturday Review* (London), 10 June 1933, p. 560.
[3] *New Statesman and Nation*, 18 February 1933, p. 181.

The London *Saturday Review*, a paper that 'puts Empire first', called these students 'handfuls of emasculate fledglings at various Universities who loudly proclaim their pacifism'.[1]

Quite naturally, Cary's novel was read as a direct contribution to the topical question of anarchy and imperialism, and as an implied criticism of American attitudes to both the League of Nations and to the old colonial empires. Quite naturally, also, Cary devoted his Preface to the Carfax edition (1952) mainly to comments on the subject of law and anarchism. The 'original American visitor', the Preface explains 'was, in short, an anarchist of the most extreme kind, but the name did not disturb her' (p. 7). As Cary himself admits there were several Americans who were 'against the Empire' but 'were also behind Wilson'. These Americans '*did* want an international law but detested imperialism'. And though they failed to 'face reality', to see that 'the world needed some power, imperial or international, [if] only to enforce the law', these anarchists had some right on their side. 'If none had ever rebelled against the law in the name of freedom, we should still be living in the stone-age under the tyranny of some ju-ju priest-king or tribal Politburo' (p. 10).

The emphasis in Cary's 1952 Preface on law and anarchy should therefore be seen as his response to the drift of comment on the novel rather than as an indication of his original and primary concern. For the novel begins and ends with more comprehensive and more important questions about Birri, civilisation and change.

To understand Cary's method and meaning, it is perhaps best to begin with his principal character, Miss Hasluck. Charles G. Hoffmann says that she is 'naïvely bound by her generalisations of life at the beginning of the novel. She attributes to the Nigerians an ideal happiness unencumbered by the artificial social and religious institutions of western civilisation; they are Rousseau's "noble savages" living in a state of natural happiness which would be destroyed by

[1] Dorothy Crisp, op. cit., p. 560.

adopting the white man's laws and customs and Christian other-worldliness.' This view, Hoffmann asserts, 'is implicitly ridiculed by the description of the Africans on the first page, long before it is expressed by Marie some pages later'.[1]

This assessment is true to a large extent. Of these Africans, one is 'a gloomy-looking horse boy' who had been discharged 'for eating his horse's rations' (p. 13); another is 'an old brown gentleman in a turban' who is shown darning 'a green silk stocking with brown wool'. Beside them are 'eight of the worst blackguards in Gwanki'. Henry, their distinguished and natural leader, has just come out of gaol 'for robbing carriers' women'. He is 'a miserable-looking object, not much more than the dirty framework of a Negro hung with the rags of an old khaki shirt whose flaps in front and behind dangled in ribbons over the greasy legs of a pair of dress trousers. His hat was bright green felt shaped like a pudding basin; a lady's hat begged from Hasluck' (p. 14). The setting in which they appear is equally uninspiring. Gwanki, we are told, 'was the loneliest port on the Niger. It consisted of a broken piece of gaspipe rail and two old planks rotting at the edge of a mud bank. Its liveliest inhabitants for three hundred and sixty days in a year were a couple of baboons scratching themselves in a human manner and barking at a distant fisherman; or two crocodiles half awash in steaming ooze' (p. 15). Hoffmann's conclusion is thus right: Marie's idea of noble savages in a state of natural happiness is ridiculed even by the first few pages of the novel.

But this conclusion is only a half-truth. Just as Cary undermines the romanticism of Miss Hasluck by his selection and presentation of a sparse and even brutal side of local environment, so also does he ridicule the other characters. Cottee is introduced to us as '*Redhead*', the nickname the natives had for him 'because his hair was yellow'. In his affair with Marie he looked a fool to the natives: 'Every day Redhead and she marched together and at night they passed

[1] 'Joyce Cary's African Novels: "There's a War on"', *South Atlantic Quarterly*, LXII (Spring, 1963), p. 233.

among the boys' huts arm in arm, strolling towards the forest. Sometimes they quarrelled and then the man behaved like a bridegroom, apologising and paying compliments until the woman was once more laughing' (p. 14). The Africans recognised the impending collapse of that relationship. But while it lasted they wished it well if only because 'it was agreed by everybody that Cottee loved and desired Hasluck' (p. 14).

Gore, the local British judge, is equally unimpressive. The natives called him 'Stork' because of his 'long thin legs, his long neck and long face and long beak'. And as he came up and ordered these blackguards to 'clear out', the crowd 'scattered before him, laughing, to gather again five minutes later, a yard or two closer to the tent' (p. 15).

The other Englishmen in the area are Jukes and Dr Dollar. Jukes is described as 'a little yellow old man with gold spectacles and a thin beard'. He resembled, so says the novel, 'a last century don even in his voice and polite nervous manners' (p. 16). We first see him at the top of the slope 'scuttling about like a scalded rat hunting for a lost load' (p. 16). Dollar had a 'heavy pale face', which, 'thrust under a patched net of white muslin, hung in the air like a conjurer's illusion'. When he was introduced to Bewsher, he 'turned his green eyes and gave a slight nod' (p. 27).

Since there is, thus, no very sharp contrast established between the whites and the blacks, Hoffmann's observation needs to be applied with some care, for 'even the whites', the novel says, 'were miserable' (p. 16). Indeed Cary's emphases seem intended to counteract the force of any such generalisation as Hoffmann's. Thus Gore, as he made for a new scene of disturbance, 'remembered with sardonic amusement the Yankee woman's remark, almost the only one he had heard from her lips, that Gwanki reminded her of home, "everybody just worried to death." He liked that piece of cynicism from the worried little woman because it gave him a glimpse of feelings very like his own' (pp. 18–19). His was a cynicism, moreover, for which there was some foundation. Earlier, as he climbed the bank 'for the fiftieth time after holding court of pie powder between three screaming women armed with each other's faggots', Gore thought that he had never seen 'so many miserable, worried people together, not even *in the largest and richest capitals*' (p. 16; italics added).

Cary's setting and the description of his Africans do not, then, so much distinguish the Africans and ridicule the idea that they are 'noble savages' as present the comedy of their harried existence (as also that of the Englishmen) under pressure of an administrative and a physical handicap. For the scene at Gwanki is a Carian world in miniature. The problems of order—moral and political—are as complicated there as in any state. In such a world the only people who can be 'contented' are the Mallam, the senior Resident going on leave, and the Birri chiefs. For only they are free from all responsibility for order at Gwanki; and it is this freedom that gives them their composure.

Cary is quick enough to see these chiefs in particular as aloof from the confusion around them.

> The expressions of these naked warriors as they gazed upon the antics and miseries all about them were like those of aristocratic travellers in barbarian parts or visitors to the Zoo monkey house. They watched with calm, interested faces as if from another and more distinguished state of being. Beside each man, his spear, standing point downwards and ready for instant use, guaranteed that distinction (p. 19).

Their Victorian 'self-confidence and dignity', the novel says, 'was founded on a complete idea of things' (p. 19). This assessment comes through the author's own voice. If it had been Miss Hasluck's, in view of what we already know of her attitudes, we should have considered it only consistent with her persistent idealisation of Africa and Africans. If, moreover, Cary had not accounted for the composure of these chiefs in simple human terms, this comparison with 'aristocratic travellers in barbarian parts or visitors to the Zoo monkey house' would have seemed tendentious and even false. The beauty of the characterisation is that it is as generous

53

to the chiefs as it is critical of them: 'naked warriors' gazing upon 'the antics and miseries all about them' as it were from 'another and more distinguished state of being', with 'self-confidence and dignity'.

What is unique, then, in this presentation of the Birri chiefs in addition to its obviously condescending humour is Cary's willingness, we might say, to see such men as they probably saw themselves. In their world, these chiefs were men of importance and behaved as such. The confusion at the ferry point was the responsibility of Gore to resolve. 'If this steamer did not come for them, another would be found' (p. 19). This was a security none of the other Africans shared with them. 'Everyone else in Gwanki except the whites had a ten to one chance of being marooned on a mud flat twelve hours' march from the nearest village. That was why women with babies on their backs were fighting like polecats for two feet of cracked mud on the water's edge' (p. 19).

The resulting disorder among the Birri as well as among British administrators and prospectors is thus an occasion, though only on a small scale, to study how men respond to stress and uncertainty. Cary is presenting to us, in miniature, the picture of a complication which is even more various and more critical in real life. This complication involves all men because they all share in the resultant predicament. Under stress, their common humanity stands out while the cultural and class peculiarities pale into insignificance. Henry and his fellow convicts may appear cringing and suppliant, but they are not symbolic of a natural African servility. They (and the novel) have a more apposite explanation: their conduct 'would give them a free passage to Birri' (p. 19). Even so, they remain proud and fun-loving, becoming 'insolent' to Marie Hasluck and using 'double meanings' at her expense. But this was 'no wilful cruelty', the novel is careful to point out. 'They did not insult and worry her because they disliked her, but because she was weak; because the restraint of fear had been removed from them. *They were wandering men*' (p. 19; italics added). Thus the external pressure of their lives, when fully understood, explains their conduct and the dimensions of order possible in those circumstances.

It has also been said of Miss Hasluck that she evolved from 'a vague, unrealistic liberalism to a genuine grasp of African life'. Cary is accordingly thought to have kept 'the discordant attitudes in play to the very end, troubling only to complicate them further. The novel closes on a note of inconclusiveness passionately, painstakingly explored.'[1] In consequence, we are 'hard put, once again, to move from the personal construction to any form of objective truth'.[2] This conclusion clearly fails to appreciate the truth which the novel consistently illustrates—that the answer to the question 'Are the Birri noble savages?' is 'Yes and No' because the question can only be answered in that way. Indeed, Miss Hasluck's mission to Birri is unnecessary; and it is no accident that the novel opens with the Birri puzzled by the purposelessness of her visit. What could Marie be doing with the miners if she was not 'a miner or a trader or a teacher or a missionary'? One answer to this question is full of Carian irony: 'just walking. . . . All whites are like that.' The curse of the white man, according to the Mallam, is that of the wandering Jew, and the reason is that, Europeans 'have set their hearts on the vanities of the world—on wealth and power and indulgence' (p. 13), categories of vice which incriminate the prospectors, the administrators and Miss Hasluck, in that order.

This explanation would seem to bear out Miss Hasluck's claim for the natural happiness of Africans who are secure from the vice of material pursuits. It would also seem to support her because we later come to know about the harried life of the prospectors, missionaries and administrators. Jukes, for example, was said to be 'on the edge of bankruptcy, so that he could not well avoid being worried'. Cottee, too, was worried, but 'God knows what was wrong with [him]', for he appeared to have 'no responsibilities and

[1] Robert Bloom, *The Indeterminate World*, p. 50.
[2] Ibid., p. 52.

everything he could want' (p. 16). But the Africans themselves reject the Mallam's argument. By offering a 'suggestion
so obscene and droll that even the old Mallam laughed'
(p. 13), they seem to remind us that their world was nothing
so sacred, solemn or pure, so free from frivolity and indulgence as to justify the Mallam's view of the white world.

A similar statement and counterstatement occurs in the
discussion which the Africans hold about Marie's affair with
Cottee, a scandal the force of which was mitigated only by
the uncertainty among the Africans about the extent to which
it had gone. 'Whether Cottee had succeeded in the affair
before the big quarrel of the night before was a question that
had been debated all over Gwanki by dozens of carriers and
servants' (p. 14). Convinced of Marie's immorality, Henry
took the opportunity to imply the superior moral character of
Birri women. '"Miss Mah-rie is a good-for-nothing like all
these white women. Why, she slept in the same hut with
Red-head every night. And that's why he quarrelled with
her. She didn't suit him."'

This comment and this reaction could, of course, be used
to imply the moral nobility of the Birri native. But while
presenting Henry's posture of moral superiority, Cary also
saw the other side of his reasoning. Henry and the Birri were
not a sexually unimpeachable people, and their complaint
over Marie's affairs was heightened, as so often everywhere,
by Marie's apparent lack of direction, judgement or discretion. Marie was a 'good-for-nothing' because she let
Cottee take advantage of her.

Mallam defends her by arguing that it was 'because Cottee
desired her and she would not admit him' that they quarrelled. '"I was there on the mat among the loads not three
paces away and they knew I was there. But they did not
mind."' This explanation, however it might establish that
Marie was not 'good-for-nothing'—that is, not stupid—still
displeased Henry, so insistent is he on the necessity for
propriety in matters of sex. '"They have no shame, these
whites"' (p. 14). The indignation which Henry expresses

here would certainly have been further proof, could Marie endure the knowledge, that the Birri are a morally upright people. Cary makes us see from the start how Marie's own conduct undermines her position in the eyes of the people whose life she so assiduously admired. '"We don't want any perverted white bitches"' (p. 71). Miss Hasluck was in no position to teach the Birri; even though that fact, paradoxically, was further reason for her to believe in her theory of the noble savage! And if Marie might conceivably give herself to Cottee—'She said another day perhaps and he answered why not now, and she said because she must think' (p. 15)—Henry had reason to feel superior. 'He spat. "Ah! these girls are all the same—they all talk like that."'

Even more devastating is the reaction from the huge Yoruba, 'a fellow ponce with Henry' (p. 15). When he heard of Marie's admission to Cottee of past affairs with other men, he began to indulge his imagination and his ego while at the same time applying and pleading for a job. 'He called out in a laughing voice, "Mam, you want a good boy. I big strong boy fit do you good"' (p. 15).

The incident serves to show how sure of themselves this 'ponce' and his fellow burglars are and how superior they feel to every stranger around them. Cary knew that their claims were neither here nor there; that the English given the same opportunity would have had parallel comments to make about the Birri. The man who stands on one side to view the other world tends to set up a simple, but incomplete answer. When Cary was in Nigeria, as *de facto* ruler of a province, 'the natives in common greeting called [the province] my land and themselves my people'. Cary knew better than to take the compliment for a fact. 'I was like a man in a tower. He is so high that he is cut off from the people below, he can't understand what they are saying to each other, he can barely guess at what they are thinking by their gestures and the sound of the cries.'[1] It was as much to

[1] 'Christmas in Africa', in *The Case for African Freedom and other Writings on Africa* (Austin, 1962), p. 217.

challenge any attitude that does not see that Africa is as proud as it is docile, as well as to discredit Miss Hasluck's particular romanticism, that he wrote *An American Visitor*.

In the Preface, as we saw, Cary referred to an original 'American' visitor on whom some of Marie's views had been based. It is possible that Cary is suggesting that the extreme anarchism of which Marie was guilty was evidence of her Americanism. In the novel itself, Marie complains to Bewsher that Cottee had 'the silly notion that Americans are always against the government' (p. 92). Unrepentant, Cottee asks why, if that was not the case, the world was 'full of American anthropologists looking for the golden age . . . trying to find some form of society that runs itself without a government' (p. 92). Speaking about Marie, Cottee argued that if 'Allday was an Amurcan girl brought up on Freud and the fourteen points mixed in the Valentino and turned loose in a wilderness of notion salesmen and ward politicians, he'd be Bolshy' (p. 28). The trouble with Marie, he felt, was that the 'poor bitch didn't know what she was or what she wanted' (p. 28). Elsewhere Marie is described as 'the real Boston mystic, direct in descent from Emerson and Thoreau' (p. 150). In a sense, therefore, the faults of Miss Hasluck's world-view are a consequence of her American-ness, her simplistic view of the problems of human and political order.

It would be wrong, however, to take this American-ness at its face value. Cary does not. For the final meaning Cary attaches to the 'African adventure' of this 'American visitor' depends on *how wrong* Miss Hasluck was at the beginning and *how changed* in the end. To discover this we need to look closely at Cary's handling of the action and the thought of those scenes connected with the theory of government and of primitivism. This is especially useful since even Miss Hasluck had reservations about her own theories. It is useful, also, because the *extent* of her error is made apparent as much by the intrinsic wrong-headedness of her position as by the boundless and impractical enthusiasm with which she insists on it. Cary does not hide the fact that he is unsympathetic to this enthusiasm. There is no danger, therefore, that Cary's sympathies will seek to mitigate the consequences of her error. Yet, because the alternatives offered by her opponents do not recognise some of her valid perceptions, Cary had the further task of also arguing her case.

The initial conflict in the novel, it is not often noticed, is between the prospectors and the local British administration. 'The trouble in Birri was due simply to the first arrival of the miners at Lower Nok.' The Resident had issued instructions to Bewsher to 'please give all facilities' to Jukes' party and to Miss Hasluck, 'anthropologist for Birri' (p. 40). The Resident apparently saw none of the complications to arise from the presence in Birri of two groups as opposed in policy as Marie's and Jukes' are. The one group comes with a dedicated and single-minded pursuit of tin. Bewsher calls them 'tin-openers'. The other group comes with the zealot's conviction that no foreign or industrial element should be introduced into Birri society. Bewsher had asked that the entry of the prospectors into the territory be deferred until he had established the All-Birri Federation. The presence of these miners combined with the already precarious character of political and social order in Birri itself to cause the unrest and the disaster of the novel's final pages. This initial conflict has to be appreciated if we are to see that Marie's position is 'wrong' especially (perhaps, only) because it could not have withstood the pressures of a larger world force; because we know that in the world of men, tin will be dug when it is found.

Cary's miners are not evil men; they are, however, limited men. They are simple practical men, aware of the opportunities open to them for profit, and calmly indifferent to the human problems which their opportunities would introduce into Birri society. The matter is further complicated in the novel by the fact that tin does represent a big opening for the general improvement and modernisation of the country. To prevent the prospectors from entering the region, to protect the community from the callousness of materialism would

59

also amount to the creation of what Cottee called 'a human zoo'. The primary obstacle, therefore, to the miners' plans is Bewsher's plea (a judicious one in the circumstances) to have the time to consolidate his political plans for the region, not the idealistic sentiments expressed by Miss Hasluck. 'As soon as the political foundations are anything like firm. And federation might go through any day now. Then there'll have to be some sort of agreement about the laws affecting strangers —they practically haven't got any at present' (p. 41). Jukes replies to this plea with a jibe: 'So if we come back in ten or twenty years—' (p. 47).

Bewsher himself admitted that he saw the miners' case. 'I'm not blaming them. All I say is that they could do [their mining] just as well in Kamchatka or South America. There's no reason on earth why they should come to Birri and smash up my whole show' (p. 42). Accordingly, when the confrontation between the miners and Marie comes, its effect is to force the administrators, Bewsher and Gore, to support the miners (against Marie) in insisting that modernisation ought to come; and to support Marie (against the miners) that the Birri had a way of life worth preserving. The miners saw in this concession to Marie's ideas a threat to their future. To them she was 'a very dangerous agitator' (p. 27). In their kind of financial venture they could ill 'afford to have trouble'. After all, investments were involved, and their children's education, too. Marie's ideas jeopardised their financial security; even if only for that reason, they found her plea for 'self-determination for bare-arsed apes' a very 'dangerous kind of intoxicant for conceited, truculent savages like the Birri' (p. 28).

In presenting this conflict between the ideas Marie advocates and the opposite ones supported by the miners, Cary lets the burden fall on the officers whose responsibility it is to keep the peace. Bewsher, as we have seen, had different but quite legitimate reasons for opposing the entry of the miners into his province. Gore, a more cautious man, knew that Bewsher had a good case, but he would rather follow the general drift of things. Cary makes us see that Gore 'did not like his [own] position any more than he cared for Bewsher's policy, which he thought impracticable, or his methods, which he thought undignified' (p. 42). Moreover, the miners were armed with the 'Exclusive Prospecting Licence' from London, an imperial document which 'having been registered gives a prospector sole mining rights within an area defined in it'. The Jukes party held two of these; Cottee had a third. Gore realised that he could not do much to 'kybosh the whole scheme at the same time' (p. 41). After all, the prospectors 'had spent a good deal of money on their expedition and ... one at least of their licences was in order. They would not easily be prevented from using their legal rights' (p. 41).

It is at this point, when the material claims of the miners conflict with the interests of the Birri, that Bewsher introduces a matter (which Marie herself would have loved to raise) about the possible aesthetic and moral effects of a tin mine on Birri life. Bewsher looked 'thoughtfully at Gore, "You'd rather fancy a mining camp in Birri—have you ever seen one?"' (p. 41). That is to say, Bewsher 'was not going to have Nok turned into a slum'. The reaction of the miners to this attitude is to attribute its logic to bureaucratic fuzziness. Because Gore was not willing to share their alarm and shut Marie out of Birri, they had called him a 'nincompoop' and an 'imbecile'. 'My God, this is the kind of people responsible for our safety, for the government of the Empire' (p. 27). Confronted now with Bewsher's firm opposition which Gore conveys to them, Jukes reacts in equally derisive language: 'I know of course that you young gentlemen don't understand business. . . . I'm not blaming you—you don't know any other kind of life. I quite realise that you've got to amuse yourself with something, and this Birri game is better than golf or spillikins' (p. 48).

If we see Marie's idealism as a rejection of this rather simplified and possibly cynical view of the political situation in Birri, her ideas cease to be the kind of madness they might

61

otherwise seem. Cary appropriately links the first important local opposition to the miners with a scene in which the Birri again discuss the purpose of Marie's visit. Obai had assured them that Marie was 'their friend'. But this was not assurance enough. 'Why, in that case [they argued], did she ask so many questions? And what was she doing in Nok so far from her own country?' (p. 59). They hoped Bewsher would be able to tell them when he came at the end of the month.

What follows, in that scene, is typical of Cary. Unobtrusively, and very much aware of what he himself called the tragic 'complacency, the self-satisfaction of the world'.[1] Cary presents us with a vindication of Bewsher's fears and at the same time a justification of the circumspect attitude which the natives had adopted.

> The same day that Bewsher arrived two other white men came and began to measure the fields. The Nok people were taken by surprise. The crowds that had come from the neighbouring villages of the tribe to see Bewsher stood in a close packed mass staring at the three white men in the middle of Obai's yam field.
>
> There was Bewsher with his early morning hat. . . . There was the Stork with his red-rimmed eyes and a drop of sweat on the end of his beak. . . . There was the pink-faced Redhead in beautiful white breeches and long laced-up boots (pp. 59–60).

The vindication of Bewsher's fears is shown in the construction which the people place on the incident. 'They've come to take our farms; they're putting magic to stop the yams growing—then they will say the land is no good and take it from us' (p. 60). Bewsher's arrival only a few hours before the miners and his presence in the field with them only helps to associate him with this conspiracy. The natives had good reason to believe that he had 'sold' them. The first line of action that occurred to them was to 'finish with all this foreign vermin'. But the threat was not carried out. 'No one spoke loudly or looked indignant. It was felt that this matter was complicated, it required reflection' (p. 60).

[1] *Art and Reality*, p. 185.

The incident is perhaps the shortest single fictional exposé of workaday exploitive imperialism. The picture of Cottee and Gore, armed with an 'EPL' issued in London and registered at Gore's office, measuring claims around Obai's yam field, is embarrassingly comic. Beneath its literal truth is a criticism of the assumption which had fortified the miners in their drive to enter the province. Behind their action, too, is a disregard of the wishes or feelings of the local owners of the land, the arrogance of the miners' assumption that the legality of the imperial 'ELP' eliminated all the human problems involved in the appropriation of Birri land. It is to this last fact that Bewsher alluded in his angry outburst at Gore: '"How the hell would you like a lot of Birri apes digging in your back garden and telling you to take compensation or leave it?"' (p. 62).[1] The uprising which followed this incident, we must note, did not arise from Marie's 'self-determination'. Cary's juxtaposition of incidents has made that conclusion impossible. The Birri did not need Marie's education to resent the expropriation of their back-gardens. Cary could have seen the problem as an administrative one; he could have seen it simply as a moral problem. Cary lets us see it principally as a human problem, involving and transcending both morality and expertise. *Human*, as it affects the men whose duty it is to administer the interests of men, and *a problem* of values as it affects the Birri, whose world this innovation will eventually change.

But though Marie is not the source of this initial conflict, she it is who gives the conflict its serious and ideal formulation. In so doing, she makes the mistake of all idealists. She denies the practical complexity of the problem at hand, and

[1] There is no small irony in the fact that subsequently Bewsher himself, who had so clearly seen the injustice of the Licence, would be obliged, as administrator, to appease the crowd by announcing that the whites 'were visitors come to admire your country, and [that] intelligent, well-mannered people like the Birri' would surely know how to welcome 'their guests' (p. 63). This compromising situation is the typical lot of Cary's conscientious and imaginative administrators. They have to save the world from its own complications, without hamstringing it.

simplifies the solutions for the ensuing crisis.[1] Not content with exhorting Obai not to let the white man 'spoil your land or take you away to work for them'—a plea which would seem justified in part by later developments in Nok—Marie went to the extreme of questioning the usefulness of all material prosperity. '"What do you need money for, Obai? You have what money can't buy—happiness that the whites can't get for themselves with any money because of their bad education"' (p. 33).

The proposition she states is a continuation of a theme announced early in the novel. Mallam had attributed the vagrant and prospecting spirit of the whites to their loss of the 'peace of God', their total devotion of 'heart and soul on the vanities of the world—on wealth and power and indulgence' (p. 13). This statement would seem to coincide with that which Marie now offers: '"Do people value the air they breathe and the water of the river? Don't they say these are things we'll always have and the others will be added to them? The whites said that and now they live in towns with bad air and no rivers"' (p. 33). There is a simple logical *non sequitur* in her argument, but Cary does not use it against her. Rather, in the simple but far-reaching method of his best work, Cary shows how both Mallam and Marie are repudiated by the realities of the world of men and hardship. Just as Mallam's audience of Africans had quickly interrupted his 'pious edification', so now Henry listened to Marie's argument 'with astonishment'. For him it was all a joke and a madness. 'He looked round at the Birri with a knowing grin as if to say, "You don't swallow this stuff, do you?"' (p. 34). Even more significant is the fact that the Birri had not even heard a word of Marie's argument. They were 'gazing at the water with the wooden faces of their images . . . Uli was dreaming' (p. 34). Only Obai is impressed by Marie's

[1] This limitation in idealism is explored in detail in the second trilogy. In *The Horse's Mouth*, Cary points to the tragedy and the nobility of the idealist who knows the limitations as well as the sublimity of his idealism.

thesis; but then he is the 'fiery young stag' among them. Marie's preaching is finally thoroughly ridiculed by the very blackguard she had only recently employed *on a salary*:

> Marie was telling them not to be tempted from their villages and farms even for big pay, because it would destroy their lives.
>
> Henry grew disgusted, irritable. He tried to catch Mam's eye to let her see that she had at least one auditor who knew what was what, who had travelled in the civilisation of the great Nigerian world.
>
> But she did not see him. She was excited, eager, like a juju man filled with his spirit which makes him sing, pray, dance. Her face was like Obai's, and Henry thought, 'Two fools, two savages. That's why the other whites won't have anything to do with her' (p. 34).

Bewsher would have agreed with part of the 'common sense' of Henry's attitude, and seen that the thing to avoid was not employment but its ill-effects; not the white man but his complications. Bewsher himself had initiated a rather controversial project called the Kifi Scheme: one of his 'darlings on which he had spent a good deal of his own money. It was intended to be the foundation of a most elaborate structure which had so far not got beyond foundations and a pigeon-hole at Kumana' (p. 91). A disciple of Plunkett, Bewsher (like Cary before him)[1] believed that the individual ownership of land was 'a product and necessity of better farming, and co-operation on the Irish model for marketing and supplies' (p. 91). While, therefore, Bewsher opposed the tin-scheme, he was quite aware that he was preventing the creation of some useful economic base for his province. What Bewsher was doing, then, was to settle for an economic lag in order to foster the political stability he so desperately needed.

His choice naturally raised the question, implicit in Marie's romanticism, of the relative value of the material well-being which mining might bring and the social stability and cohesion which its absence would make possible. Cary's answer, as always, is in the form of short scenes, even anecdotes. In

[1] Wright, *Joyce Cary*, p. 24.

one of them, Obai, who is elated by the nationalist fervour inspired by Marie's prodding, refuses the gift of whisky and tea (modern innovations) which Henry, the apostle of material necessity, presents to Uli and himself.

> Uli, who would have liked to accept them, submitted to his friend's ruling only under protest. He said even twenty minutes later as they passed in single file through flickering brown and green shadows from the forest 'That drink is good' (p. 50).

This acknowledgement that whisky and tea, even if not Birri drinks, are nevertheless good, makes Obai's idealism ('It's not a Birri drink, but a white man's drink') a mere pettiness, a constriction of the heart and the imagination, a limitation of his own powers. Uli was not the poorer man for acknowledging the quality of whisky, nor did he enjoy his fatherland the less.

> His eyes darted here and there among the trees, noticing the smallest indications of human or animal passage, his ears were alert to the minutest sounds, all his faculties were rejoicing. He, too, was keenly conscious of this delightful time, in the cool of the evening, when he was home again in Birri among his own trees, under his own sky, among his own spirits (p. 51).

In another episode, Cary describes the pastoral character of Birri life. The river bank, he noted, was the children's playground, the young people's 'club'. 'Here they played all day at hunting, fishing, marriages, wars, shops, built huts for themselves, and planted farms of broken palm leaf bedded in mud; danced, sang, and rolled shrieking a hundred times an hour down the steep bank into the water. Nok children had no clothes to tear or make dirty and no restriction of noise' (pp. 157–158). These children, the novel says, 'were the happiest children on earth, *in spite of fever, smallpox, dysentery and a dozen other diseases which killed half of them in the first five years*. For dying was no trouble' (p. 168; italics added). Cary's point is, of course, to show up both the truth and the inadequacy of Marie's romanticism. Clean air and rivers the Birri may have, and should keep; happiness, too. They still needed to reduce nature's ills and the fevers and diseases that killed half their children. 'Poverty', Cary stated in *The Case for African Freedom*, 'does not bring sympathy, only ignorance, disease, superstition.'[1] Cary had argued the same case in *Power in Men*, almost directly against Marie's disparagement of the relevance of money to happiness and liberty: 'A hundred good sentiments declare that the poorest man with liberty is still a king . . . I do not mean that money alone is the measure of liberty. . . . But for the mass of men, with which alone a standard can deal, poverty is a direct restraint on liberty.'[2]

Without meaning to be generous to the Birri, Cottee is spokesman in the novel for this hard truth. Ridiculing Marie's notion of a Providentially-ordered society where Nature looked after everything and made the world safe 'for Beudy (caricaturing Marie), truth, goodness for ever and ever while you sit in your armchair and admire the view' (p. 92), Cottee interpreted Marie's ideas as equivalent to not letting the Birri have any money to play with 'in case they buy the same sort of things that we find indispensable— clothes and metal pots and hats and so on' (p. 94); as if 'civilised dress and amusements were bad in themselves. . . . Natives who wore trousers and went to the cinema instead of hunting lions mightn't be so picturesque as the naked savages, but they'd be happier' (p. 96). His conclusion is debatable, but his general case is incontrovertible: material well-being could indeed improve the condition of African life.

The brutal fact which the novel drives home, however, is that in order to advocate such a common-sense view of material well-being without reservations, one had also to have a turn of mind willing to reject all non-material idealism. That is to say that Cottee was able to believe in the pre-eminence of material prosperity because, as he himself said, there was scarcely a limit to what 'given effrontery, money and the proper jargon' a man could do. 'If his Paré flotation

[1] *The Case for African Freedom*, p. 122.
[2] *Power in Men* (Seattle, 1963), pp. 77–78.

came off, he would be a rich man' (p. 236). Poor old Gore would then be 'rotting on a twopenny pension in some third-rate suburb . . . and we started together' (p. 236). Good living never blunted the sensibilities. 'A dash of hoggery now and then may even improve and refine the artistic reactions' (p. 236). This worldly wisdom, not so different from Henry's, directly limits the general validity of Cottee's philosophy. He was right, originally, in recognising the increase of power of action or freedom which material prosperity could bring; but wrong in his scorn for any idealism which did not first pay court to the pragmaticism of wealth. Cary studies an exemplar of this pragmaticism in Henry, the chief exponent of that view among the Birri.

Henry had rejected Marie's mystical attitude to wealth. In his newly acquired wealth, Henry 'did not only act like a master but he looked like a master', with his 'new English hat over his left ear, his silver-mounted walking stick twirling in his hand' (p. 157). Thus secure from the daily trials of poverty, Henry even seemed to become a more genial man, in contrast to the robber he had once been. In the tradition of 'civilised men everywhere in the world of cash values, his good nature, his sympathies had increased with prosperity and he was everybody's friend' (p. 157). At the same time, however, he was beginning to worship the predatory ethics of the prospectors, taking his cue from what he considered the code of most civilised people. Among such people, 'men are not afraid to take what they want, and they would laugh at all the rules which tie us like sheep' (p. 163). In the Sudan, for example, 'everybody did what he liked'. 'Everybody was free and happy and able to acquire riches and to defy all rulers, chiefs, ju-jus and laws—everybody, that is, with any intelligence and pluck' (p. 163).

Henry had just that kind of intelligence and that kind of pluck, and afforded Cary a parallel to the divergence between the careers of Gore and Cottee which we noted earlier. By the end of the novel, Henry, in his own way, is the kind of successful man Cottee would become: 'the dignified

Henry with his grave, important look and his silver-mounted walking stick' (p. 205). Just as Cottee had mused on the gap between his prosperity and Gore's, so now Uli ponders the great change between Henry and himself.

> He remembered Henry on the Kunama road, a miserable, starved wretch ready to lick the feet for a cigarette or a bowl of broth; now he was a man of power and wealth. Look at his fat legs, his fat chin, his great soft belly. What a clever rascal he was. It was wonderful. It was good to look at Henry (p. 205).

Henry had become a success. Having made huge profits from the war 'rake-off and the wages of the dead, sick and wounded', he, appropriately, opened a store near Cottee's Paré minefield and began 'a splendid trade in condemned tinned meats slightly blown, second-hand caps and trousers, aphrodisiacs and smuggled gin. Abortions sixpence' (p. 233).

Only thus indirectly, then, does Cary raise Marie's romanticism from the abstract argument it might have been to the many-sided human problem it is. Marie was wrong, as we have shown, in her denial of the power for good in material things. But she was right in her fears that such well-being would inevitably mean the destruction, or at least the weakening, of some of the richer values of a non-industrialised society. This inevitability is the burden of Cottee's and Gore's final soliloquies. The irony is that the prospectors who contended that modernisation had to proceed at any cost also resented the introduction of new 'ideas' (otherwise called 'self-determination') into the country. In arguing that self-determination was 'a dangerous kind of intoxicant for savages' (Obai had argued that whisky was a similar intoxicant), the miners were joining forces with those who, as Cary put it, argued that the African was 'a light-hearted but also a light-headed sub-man, a born helot and parasite'.[1]

Their error was as glaring as Marie's, and so needed equal refutation. On the one hand, there are the prospectors, in search of tin, and unconcerned with the consequences of their

---

[1] *The Case for African Freedom*, p. 24.

search for social and moral order among the Birri. 'Co-operation', Cottee conceded, 'was all very nice. Let 'em co-operate by all means. He quite agreed that they were probably ideal material for co-operation. But that wasn't the point' (p. 96). On the other side was Marie, quixotically seeking to preserve the values of the Birri world, even at the expense of material progress. '"In Birri there is nothing of what we in America and in Europe call civilisation. . . . Among the Birri you do not find anybody who is tired of life or troubled about his soul. You do not find any uplifters, prohibitionists, Calvinists, Marxists, Freudians, nympho-maniacs, sadists, yogi standing on their heads or fundamenta-lists sitting on their tails, to tell you what you ought to do and to curse you, murder you or poison you if you don't do it. This simplifies life a whole lot and leaves the Birri time for such primitive pastimes as dancing and singing, making poems . . . hospitality and happiness"' (p. 60). Between the miners and Marie, between material and non-material ideal-ism stand Gore and Bewsher; Gore nearer the miners just as Bewsher is closer at heart to Marie. They want the good of the Birri by a systematic preservation of Birri institutions and the eventual introduction of modern amenities and modern industries.

These are the three forces in *An American Visitor* which, together, condition the form and the nature of Cary's qualifications to, and affirmations of, Marie's evangelism, and of the more positive moral and social understanding which Cary deduces from the situation. He had made Uli speculate on this ultimate significance early in the novel. When pressed by Gore to tell what the problem was in Birri, why there was so much anxiety and panic, he could not find words to tell it.

> The question it seemed was not a thing you could take in one hand, like a spear shaft, but a whole mass of things, a forest, a web of foliage and tie-tie.
> It wasn't only about farms, about the juju, about law, nationalism, about strangers, whisky, war, money, Christianity, trade, soldiers, and the rights and the powers of the white men and the authority

of their God, it was about himself too. Where was he, what was he? What had happened to him? (pp. 80–81).

Uli's questions cannot be answered; for his dilemma and that of the Birri nation is a tragic anomaly. What that dilemma signifies in the long run is asserted by the novel in the anecdote of the old Russian lady and her precious china smashed to pieces by ignorant drunken soldiers.

> It wouldn't have been any good to tell that old lady that beauty would not perish with her Sèvres—that the roots of beauty were as indestructible and as fertile as life itself—that though cruelty and lies might carry all before them for a time, they had never yet succeeded in abolishing the things of the spirit. . . . The greater a period, the stronger the allegiance and interdependence of its human parts—the more difficult its liquidation, the more painful for these fragments (p. 235).

The crisis in *An American Visitor*, then, is the crisis of all change, the effects of any attempt to resist a force which came 'with all the whole drive of the world behind it, bringing every kind of gaudy toy and easy satisfaction' (p. 234). The novel, therefore, refuses to press a simple thesis. 'I was asked about the *American Visitor*', Cary noted in his Prefatory essay to the Carfax edition of the novel. 'So what? And this is all the answer one can give. There is no rule. The situation in family life as in politics is always unique; it has to be dealt with by the imagination, by a creative effort of the mind. And since only individuals possess imagination, there is always need of the individual ruler whoever he or she is called' (p. 11).

The result, in *An American Visitor*, is a partial destruction of the age-old symbols of 'primitive goodness' and 'barbaric savagery'. Because Cary had to see his characters as people fulfilling themselves in their several ways, he could concentrate on presenting the tragedy as well as the comedy of any resulting culture-conflict, and do so, moreover, without imposing on it a pattern of destructive consequences deriving from prior conceptions of 'European' and 'African' psychology. Thus, though Obai, Uli and Henry are still part of their native Africa, they remain different kinds of people. They each show the effects of their contact with European life. But none of them lives in terror of himself as a result; when they seem to, it is actually because, like Obai, they seek to absorb it into the idea of their own private and national life.

Uli, as we saw, recognised the terrible consequences of his cultural dislocation. 'Where was he, what was he? What had happened to him? Had he committed a sin worthy of punishment? Or would nothing happen to him if he escaped Enuke's brothers?' (p. 81). And Uli knew that Gore, though well-meaning, would never understand the extent of that dislocation because he was necessarily outside Birri society; because the change challenged, not merely the forms of the social order Uli was used to, but also the norms of Uli's personal order, his very identity. Thus in Uli's case, the 'war' remained deep and furious, without becoming stereo-typical and spectacular. It takes Cottee till the end of the novel to come to a recognition of this fact; even then, his distrust of idealism enables him to escape the temptation to attempt a sentimental disquisition on it. He does see, however, that the dislocation had public and personal implications, both of them crucial.

> 'Why should everything go to pot at once, the sound and the splendid as well as the bad? Why not keep the good and reform the rest? . . . These things you are destroying can't be replaced in a hurry and they may be necessary to you. Loyalty, truth, tolerance, kindness, even modesty will be wanted again—and you will enjoy the graces of life as you know what they are' (pp. 234–235).

Cary saw that the rearrangement of norms in Birri would not allow for discrete reform; for the new order 'came with the whole drive of the world behind it, bringing every kind of gaudy toy and easy satisfaction'. Cary could show this because in *An American Visitor* he did not seek, as Conrad might have done, to look at the face of Africa in order to see in it the physical correlative to his metaphysical concerns over civilisation and savagery, imperial idealism and Victorian high culture. Though aware of these concerns, Cary wrote primarily to record the scepticism, the joy in life, the embarrassment at the responsibilities of life typical of those who knew the limitations of their own lives and sought, nevertheless, to make the best of them. Uli, dragging himself behind Bewsher before the attack on Goshi, moved 'like one joint in a centipede'. But, as the novel also indicates, 'to himself he seemed released, free, released from futility, free of boredom; once more Uli of Nok, a somebody in the world, his own world' (p. 205). Cary's message remained a humane and a humanising one.

4: Demons of Africa

Cary says in one of his letters that his African novels dealt with one theme: the 'war between incompatible ideas'. At one time he meant to call this series of novels ' "There's a war on", as a general title; or something of that kind.'[1] It has been argued from this evidence that the African novels were 'intended as a multiple novel, having a unifying concept—the war between different cultures in Africa—to give structural unity. Each separate novel dramatises at least one major "battle" of this war so that the whole is a complex portrayal of the revolution that took place in the early decades of the twentieth century (and is still taking place today) in Africa.'[2]

The idea of a planned series of African novels is an attractive one. It is not clear at what date the idea of such a plan first came to Cary. In his Preface to *The African Witch* he tells us: 'After I finished *An American Visitor*, I decided to write no more books about Africa. I was actually planning *Castle Corner*, to cover a wider scene (and above all, to avoid the African setting . . .), when my agents asked me for another African book.'[3] This would suggest that the idea of a series could not have occurred to Cary until after the two earlier novels had been written, and perhaps not until *The African Witch* was on the way to being published.

[1] Charles G. Hoffmann, 'Joyce Cary's African Novels: "There's a War on"', *South Atlantic Quarterly*, LXII (Spring, 1963), p. 230.

[2] Ibid., p. 230.

[3] Prefatory Essay to *The African Witch*, Carfax ed. (London, 1951), p. 11. Subsequent references are to this edition and will be cited in parentheses after quotations.

In *The African Witch*, Cary does deal with a 'war'. 'The attraction of Africa', Cary claims, 'is that it shows . . . wars of belief, and the powerful often subconscious motives which underlie them, in the greatest variety and also in very simple forms. Basic obsessions, which in Europe hide themselves under all sorts of decorous scientific or theological uniforms, are there seen naked in bold and dramatic action' (p. 10). This assumption meant, in effect, that his material had to be selected and presented to show this naked, bold and dramatic action; in order to underscore, not so much the actual life of Africa, as the war of cultures within it. This emphasis, as Cary realised, would require 'a certain kind of story, a certain violence and coarseness of detail, almost a fabulous treatment, to keep it in its place' (p. 11).

In a sense, this is an un-Carian procedure: his emphases were always on how men, in a variety of circumstances and even in the thick of war, carved out personally satisfying lives for themselves. That the result of his method in *The African Witch* might be tendentious, Cary himself suspected, for even in the Preface written several years later, he speaks of one of the difficulties he faced in writing the novel. He had to 'do justice and to give truth, in a medium which is at once the only vehicle of truth as an experience, and at the same time highly subjective and irrational; that is to say, the truth of art which is true because it conveys the feeling without which facts are insignificant and delusive, but at the same time personal to each reader' (p. 11). *The African Witch*, as Cary himself tells us, was meant to 'show certain men and their problems in the tragic background of a continent still little advanced from the Stone Age, and therefore exposed, as no other, to the impact of modern turmoil. An overcrowded raft, manned by children who have never seen the sea would have a better chance in a typhoon' (p. 12). *An American Visitor* also gave that same impression of African life, but it did not isolate it, radically and permanently, from human life in the way *The African Witch* does. Nor did it give that impression at the expense of a realisation of the actual and creative life of its people. *An American Visitor*, that is, did not pre-judge its own evidence.

The African Witch is, accordingly, an unhappy combination of two styles: the one seeking, like Conrad, to mythologise a conflict of forces and values; the other, in the spirit of Cary's best fiction, trying to understand the actual lives of the men and women involved in that conflict. The combination is unhappy precisely because the first style denies the assumptions on which the second depends. The second style with which the novel begins tries to recognise Coker's and Aladai's sense of themselves and of their situation in the world of white colonial administrators, under whom they still manage to hold their heads high. 'The two young men laughed together at the remark made by one of them, and the spectacle of their nonchalance, their gaiety, infuriated the little white woman, so gentle and timid by nature that her life in civilised Rimi was a nightmare to her' (p. 15). The first style, on the other hand, intent on mystery and thesis, speaks of the 'subtlety' of Aladai's 'Hamitic blood' and of Coker's theology, 'the geyser, the hot fountain shot out of 'primaeval mind' (p. 50), as better explanations of their conduct than the search for self-assertion with which the novel begins. It is indicative of the power and attractiveness of this style that Aladai is finally overwhelmed less by fact than by blood, by 'one of those obsessions that seize the half educated, the Negroes'. It is indicative of its limitations that it is only in his second style that Cary can record the scenes of domestic and childhood life, and all the most penetrating and human incidents of the novel.

The 'war' or conflict which Cary deals with in *The African Witch* is fought on four 'fronts'. The first of these, and very important since its outcome affects all the other three, is religious. Elizabeth is the African Witch, and she is shown as the epitome of native religious sentiment, in its pagan, non-Muslim manifestation. She is a powerful and formidable figure both in her own person and by virtue of her office:

She almost filled the opening, which framed her with the sunlight streaming into the yard behind. She was a woman who seemed, in her height and proportions, bigger than the largest and most powerful men. In fact, she was probably about five foot ten in height, and fifteen or sixteen stone in weight—not of fat, but of bone and muscle.

In feature she was like her brother Louis, 'but more negro, energetic, and sensual. . . .'

She wore a black velvet cloth tightly wrapped round her below the armpits, and almost touching the ground. This cloth made her seem like a moving pillar. Its dead black, which appeared greenish in the sun contrasted with living tints of the black flesh, which changed at each motion flashing copper, golden, blue-brown in different angles of light.

The woman was far gone with child, but this, in her slow movement, added to her monumental dignity (p. 32).

The power she wields and the assurance with which she wields it are central to Cary's interest in her; and though he compares this assurance to that of the European woman who 'talks of her intuition', or of the gardener who speaks of his 'growing hand', it is clear that Cary meant the reader to identify Elizabeth's with a very high order of primitive confidence. Elizabeth, as ju-ju priest, 'had every reason to believe in her power, for she saw the visible effects of them. Every day women blessed her for making them bear, for bringing them good trade, good husbands, and men thanked her for curing their sore throats' (p. 33). Cary insists that Elizabeth believed in her own gods. After hearing the 'evidence' about Osi's being a witch, Elizabeth ceased to have a 'conscious will' of her own. 'She put from her mind all the evidence that she had heard. She placed herself under control of the ju-ju spirit, and now she felt that spirit swelling and spreading through her whole body. She released her muscles . . . she softened her legs, bending them at the knees, making her flesh soft for the penetration of the spirit' (p. 34). Later, when Akande Tom, flaunting his Christian conversion, calls Elizabeth 'you damn witch' and leaves her, Elizabeth 'was surprised'.

> She returned thoughtfully to her yard. Afterwards she went to the ju-ju house and made medicine for Tom's return.
>
> This medicine, sold to many women in Rimi, obliges a husband's return within so many days, on pain of death. The death is by wind. The man, wherever he is, swells up and dies in great pain (p. 151).

Cary's irony is heavy here; for just as he points to the fact of faith, so he undermines it by showing that 'the news that medicine has been made for a certain man's return is always broadcast. Elizabeth and her assistants take care of that, for it usually brings the man back at once, unless he has succeeded in getting an antidote at some other ju-ju' (p. 151). Cary does not, however, study the nature or the authenticity of the conviction with which she operated as witch. Instead he concentrates on the consequences of that conviction, and on the implications of her conduct for the religious conflict which involves Coker, Aladai, Schlemm and the British officials.

Cary points out the nature of Elizabeth's opposition to the Christians and to the Muslims whom she hated 'almost as much as Christians' especially as Salé had threatened her ju-ju (p. 36). The conflict is not, as one might have expected, between one faith or one theology and another, but between what might be regarded as ignorance and primitivism on the one hand, and common sense and Christian 'decency' on the other. In the Preface to *The African Witch*, Cary refers to William James's *Varieties of Religious Experience* as 'one of the most absorbing books in the world'; and finds in it support for his probing of the sources of a people's religious 'way of life'. Whether we trace such a way of life to such simple terms as 'love and hate, curiosity, ambition, duty and pride, [we] are already deep . . . in metaphysics, in the science of the soul, or whatever synonym you may choose for that central activity' (p. 10), this was to be Cary's assumption in the treatment of Brown, in *To Be A Pilgrim*, and of Preedy, in *The Captive and the Free*. In both cases, the religious imagination, expressing itself in rather unconventional, even violent, religious exercise, is nevertheless allowed that benefit of the doubt which one had to grant, if one believed that such a religious imagination was not necessarily the product of a morbid or psychotic condition.

In *The African Witch*, Cary does not quite use his Jamesian formula in this way, for he identifies the imagination supporting Elizabeth's religion with the imagination of all Africa. In consequence Cary's examination of Elizabeth's religion is not used to throw light on Elizabeth's peculiar religious imagination and character but, as it were, to support a generalisation on the connection between ju-ju and African (or negro) psychology. For if Elizabeth's faith is the faith of all Africa, and if this faith is as ingrained in the mentality of Africans as are Africa's forests and her beasts, the explanation for ju-ju also explains the character of Africans. Hence the contrasts which are established between Elizabeth's ju-ju and the other religions in the novel serve, as it were, to emphasise the extent of Africa's distance from the rational.

Coker is another side of the non-Muslim African religious imagination. Cary sees differences between the pagan and the Muslim values of the North. Muslim rulers, for example, 'contemplate, and enjoy, waiting for paradise'. For the pagan ruler, however, 'there was only one world':

> One lived among men, trees, and beasts. One reckoned with them, handled them, fought them, loved them; and, when one died, one was born again a man, a tree, or a beast, to begin again with loving, fighting, and striving for the glory and the honour of creatures.
>
> A pagan is alive to the last jump of his pulse. If he is bad, he dies bad; if he is good, he dies good. But the Mohammedan saint lives only to the glory of God (p. 178).

If pagan Africa was this different from the Muslim, it was even more different from the ideal of Christianity. In Coker, Cary found his example of a confluence of the religion of Elizabeth and that of Christ. According to Cary's Preface to the novel, Coker was begun as the study of the 'watch-tower movement' and other primitive sects derived from various sources (p. 9). In the novel, Coker becomes a preacher only because 'he did not like the confined life of a booking-office'.

79

He also finds that 'his personal creed did not fit any of the local churches. He therefore set up his own church in Rimi'. But Coker is not a mere opportunist for Cary makes him suddenly a man of power. 'Coker gave himself to his powerful spirit by speech' (p. 50).

The forms which his preaching takes reveal the nature of Cary's interest in him. His phrases, we are told, 'had a local twist—like Catholicism in Italy, France, America, or the English Church service in Kent, Ulster, Wales' (p. 50). Coker's 'local twist' was the emphasis on blood. 'His key word was blood, but it appeared in different connections: blood of Jesus—blood of sacrifice—blood of the wicked man—blood of the sinner—the baptism of blood.' His doctrine was not socialist or communistic in any intellectually-derived sense of the word. The 'geyser' of his mind,

> uttered pure original communism, the brotherhood of the pack and the herd, expressed in fraternal love for the like, in hatred for the unlike, sealed in the magical properties of blood.
>
> Blood-love, blood hatred, were the ethics of Coker's religion (p. 50).

Again, in the Preface, Cary had called Coker, a 'hysterical enthusiast' and one would have expected that the treatment which he would receive would be parallel to that given Brown and Preedy. In fact, however, Cary could not have given Coker the same serious sympathy he accorded those other religious enthusiasts without subverting the tendency of his Conradian style in favour of his indigenous voice. For Coker had to represent, not simply a single example of religious enthusiasm, but a deeper African malady. Coker's religious inconsequence had to be a symbol of Africa's 'morbid psychology and primitive religion' (p. 209).

In other words, Cary meant to present Coker's religious mission, not as an authentic expression of religious feeling however untenable, but as a manifestation of the inevitable corruption of Christian faith at the hands of primitive and blood-oriented savages. Before his death, Coker is made to emphasise this fact:

Coker picked up some round object in a bag, and held it at arm's length, his mouth was like a crater, and his voice panted, 'He gave his blood—not for white man alone—not for black man alone— and——'

The object was Schlemm's head. . . . Aladai had known perfectly well that Coker's ju-ju was Schlemm's head, but he had not wanted to admit it (pp. 287–288).

What Coker represents here is neither the regular variety of religious experience, a faint reminder of an earlier age of European Christian fanaticism nor of the intoxicated faith of the young Aissa in *Aissa Saved*, but a mongrel faith.[1] 'Such a religion is pre-human even in its ritual of blood. Beasts fear blood, and drink blood. It has a special significance for them' (p. 209). Cary does not give Coker's faith an independent realisation because Cary's idea of 'war' required Coker's faith to have its roots in the witchcraft of Elizabeth. 'Coker's slogan was, "Africa for Christ", but his conception, if you can describe his mental processes as such, was a kind of bloody sacrifice. Africa would offer herself up to Christ, in blood—not only the blood of the whites, but her own' (p. 209).

What makes Cary's powerful counterpointing of pagan and Christian religious expressions difficult to accept in *The African Witch*, then, is that it is thesis-ridden. Thus, though it would be easy to accept the primary contrast between Christian and pagan values as they operate on Coker, it becomes difficult to do so when the value of the term 'Christian' fluctuates from essence to mere form; when, that is, Christianity is no longer a specific religious model for a way of life but a label for any agreeable way of life.[2] It is in this latter sense, for example, that Captain Rubin must have

[1] It is a minor but interesting supporting fact that Coker is a mulatto.

[2] Cf. Cary's comment on Bewsher's Christianity in *An American Visitor* (Carfax ed., 1952, p. 130): 'He's not a Christian. He's what Frank Cottee calls Church. He goes to Church as a kind of political duty. He thinks of God as a kind of head of the religion and ethical department and the Holy Spirit is the district inspector going round the sub-offices checking up the staff work.'

meant his compliment to his pagan horse-boy, whom he called a 'real Christian. "See him handle The Kraken"' (p. 128).

In an even more general sense, all the Europeans of the novel are 'Christian', which means, not that they had any theological or intellectual faith in Christianity, but that they are Englishmen. And because they are English and civilised, no moral problems arise, no religious war involves them. The result is that the religious fanaticism of Africa finds a counterpart not in the faith of the European population, but in that of the German-American, Dr Schlemm, 'a real good chap' (p. 127). By this compliment, it was meant merely that nobody had anything against him, and that he was quite unlike the typical 'mish' (p. 127). 'Why was Schlemm so popular? He was not a back-slapper. He did not drink or smoke, or attempt to be one of the boys. He would sit in the Scotch club, but he did not tell funny stories, and his presence stopped others from telling them' (p. 128). What made him 'popular' were the same qualities that had made Captain Jones well-liked before his invalidation: 'fine manners, a complete lack of chicane, moral repose (in Jones' case only after his first whisky of the day) based upon a sure faith (Jones believed in the British Empire), and reserve or moral dignity' (p. 129). These together made him a 'real' Christian.

> It was worth noticing the adjective 'real'. For Sergeant Root (who used the word in admiration of Schlemm) was a real gentleman . . . not simply a person of good class and accent and polite education (p. 128).

This definition of Schlemm's 'Christianity' only applied to his relations with the Europeans; in his role as missionary to Africa, he was a Christian in quite another sense. In that other sense, he was a martyr, a Victorian Christ so committed to the salvation and the social good of Africa that he is often oblivious of the political and social upheavals which his presence either provoked or prolonged. Cary suggests a parallel between Schlemm and Schweitzer, to the extent, in fact, of making Schlemm cite 'that truly great man' as his

82

spiritual teacher (p. 134). What they had in common, apparently, was the religious and social conscience of a larger imperial burden. Though Schlemm's sermons were 'much too theological and philosophical', his work was 'practical and individualist. He had come to Africa to make people happier, and he dealt directly with persons.' He was, we are told, an 'optimist'. 'If he had not had faith in human nature, he could not have set out to be a missionary. It was his strength and his weakness that he could not believe in the treachery or wickedness of his beloved pupils' (p. 135).

The strength of this faith we can see. The weakness is less obvious. Because of his 'faith in human nature', Schlemm, like so many other enthusiasts, could not quite see the riddles and difficulties of political and social order, or how these affected the conduct of men. And because of the inability to see, there is the danger of that kind of political naïveté which prevents Schlemm from realising the extremity of the political and racial situations in Rimi. When he protested to the Resident about witch-burnings in the division, he was made a fool of by the pragmatic, non-idealistic Burwash and Rubin. 'Witch trials, though they may possibly occur still among the more primitive tribes, have not been known in Rimi for years. The last reported was in 1912' (p. 130). This was from Burwash's letter to Dr Schlemm. 'Do they still hunt witches?' Rubin asks him, tongue-in-cheek.

Cary did not intend Dr Schlemm to appear a fool. But by making him a 'holy' man, a man apart, Cary made him represent an incarnation of the Christian ideal in its apostolic and redemptionist spirit rather than in its everyday form. That is to say, Dr Schlemm becomes not so much a Christian as the antithesis of both African paganism and African Christianity.

> To men like Schlemm—scholars and, at the same time, Churchmen —the species represented by Coker is especially disgusting because it is at once the worst enemy of Christianity and the most difficult to tackle.
>
> Schlemm was not permitted to hate Coker, but it was difficult

not to hate a man who was capable of so much harm and did it all in Christ's name, who was completely satisfied in his ignorance (p. 131).

Cary's purpose in the novel also required that Schlemm be identified with civilisation and Europe, that his mission be diametrically and unequivocally opposed to Elizabeth's. Because Schlemm is doctor and pastor, the conflict between him and Elizabeth naturally centres on witchcraft, which he pointed out 'is still the curse of Africa. The ju-ju and the witch-doctor' (p. 130). From what we see of Elizabeth's ju-ju, his judgement is more than justified. But what the novel's dialectic makes of the conflict is different and less satisfying, as we shall now see.

In Aladai's first meeting with Judy, he had tried to brush off all compliments to Rimi 'civilisation', by insisting that 'the blood of what you call Rimi civilisation is ju-ju—so cruel and stupid'. Judy then asked:

> 'What happens to witches here?'
> 'Just what happened to yours in Europe—they kill them.'
> 'Yes, we can't boast.'
> 'Yes, you can boast,' the boy exclaimed. 'You have stopped it— you have escaped from it—by your English civilisation. And then you refuse it to us, in Rimi.'
> 'Your friend Mr Coker went to school out here, I suppose?'
> Aladai raised his brows and looked sharply at her. Then he smiled, and she, too, smiled. It was an exchange like a wink. . . .
> 'Of course, Coker is ju-ju too—it is what you call primitive religious ju-ju. But you can't say that it is so bad as Rimi ju-ju' (pp. 20–21).

What the exchange does then is not to evaluate the integrity of the religious life, in Rimi or in sixteenth-century England, but to imply the necessity for the introduction of English civilisation. At the same time it introduces, obliquely, the idea which comes out directly in Cary's Preface—that education (or 'English civilisation') might do even more harm than good. 'Education would bring in more violence, more barbarities;' the Preface says, 'it would break up what is left of tribal order, and open the whole country to the agitator' (pp. 12–13).

Again, it ought to be pointed out that Cary was not arguing against education, but against the contention that it would by itself 'abolish barbarity and violence' (p. 12). The effect of his argument in the Preface, like that of the novel in this regard, is to confuse the need for social progress with a need for Christian (or English) theology. The England that burned witches was, after all, both English and Christian. When, therefore, Akande Tom calls himself a Christian and defies (for a while) the authority of Elizabeth and dons an English suit, we become aware of the limitations of Cary's assumptions for this novel. For if the novel had to dramatise a war between ju-ju and Christianity, it could only do it by pitching white irrevocably against black; Africa against Europe. When offered whisky in *An American Visitor*, Obai had rejected it because it was 'foreign'; when in the same novel, Henry ridiculed the 'order' of his society preferring the opportunism of other lands, we saw that the conflict was between order and change, not between one fixed system and another, definitely not between Africa in its entirety and the totality of the European Christian experience.

In *The African Witch*, however, the conflict is simple and final. The suit which Tom wore to the station 'was crumpled and dirty; but had it been rags, so long as they were European rags, it would have given Tom an indescribable happiness' (p. 148). If the explanation for this frame of mind was to be found in Tom's character the matter might have been different. The pseudo-Conradian voice, however, preferred a more dramatic explanation. 'By wearing white man's clothes, it seemed to Tom's bodily and natural logic that he became one with the white ju-ju. . . . The white suit gave him such power that insults to him were no more than the chattering of monkeys; or, he a white man, the things muttered after him by riff-raff in a ditch' (p. 149). The ultimate conflict, it thus appears, is not the 'bitter war' Cary describes in the Preface, a war 'to defend those dogmatic fortresses and

85

prisons from which the warriors could no more venture their noses than primitive Negroes dare to go out at night into a strange forest, full of were-beasts and demons' (p. 10). In the religious front of this 'war', the African defenders are the hybrid Coker, the diabolic witch, Elizabeth, and the inconsequential Aladai—'the cannibal chief in the Balliol blazer' (p. 15).

In *An American Visitor*, there were two forms of order, and the novel explored their interaction. In *The African Witch*, there is Christian order on the one side and a rank disease on the other. Elizabeth's triumph at the end must then mean a triumph of barbarism over civilisation, of ju-ju against Christianity. But even this portentous end, as the novel sees it, has a more important implication than the religious one. In her success, Elizabeth can now humiliate Akande Tom, the would-be white man. After that humiliation 'even the little boys laugh at him; and he no longer tries to be a white man, or to learn book' (p. 309).

The resolution of the religious war in favour of Elizabeth is, of course, not an assertion of the *strength* of primitive religion, but of the tragic *banality* of its adherents. That is to say, the victory of Elizabeth at the end is the defeat of Africa; Africa's tragedy. 'Negro, energetic and sensual' (p. 32), Elizabeth had a 'big woman's expression' which was 'still fixed in a magnificent and imperial calmness, mixed with a little disdain' (p. 38). When she turned to speak to Judy, she did so 'majestically' (p. 38). But her royalty, the novel indicates, is diabolic, irrational and African; it is shaped, according to Aladai, from 'fear and ignorance and spite' (p. 66).

> At night the people went in a single file through the winding alleys of the *ju-ju* path. They held to each other because they were terrified of the darkness and the spirits of the place—spirits of victims, spirit of gods. They could hear them rustling and breathing softly among the leaves. At each sigh, they felt weak with fear, and this satisfied them (p. 256).

It is to the tradition of such unthinking primitive feeling

that Elizabeth's empire of darkness belongs. What her power at the end proves is the tenacity of the mentality of a people who, Rackham joked, 'haven't taken to thinking yet, and . . . don't suffer too much in their consciences, if they have any' (p. 252). The end of the religious war justifies this opinion by the ironic triumph of the symbol of that conscience-less barbarity. '"Rimi civilisation! You know that is a joke," Aladai himself tells Judy. "Think of the richness of the European people—the poetry, the music—the"—he waved his hand in the air—"the greatness of every kind. Rimi civilisation! Do you know what it is?—*ju-ju*"' (p. 24). Elizabeth—the African Witch—represents that civilisation.

The second front to the war in *The African Witch* is political. Again, it is important to see the nature of the assumptions on which Cary bases his treatment of this war. In *An American Visitor*, as we saw, there was a conflict between the European prospectors on the one hand, and the native population on the other; this conflict in turn aggravated the domestic problem of a Birri federation. In *The African Witch*, there is a different kind of confrontation. The British, whether traders or officials, cease to be regarded as a target of political hostility and become the passive and cynical agents of a disillusioned colonial system. This difference is easily seen in Aladai's letter of protest to the Resident:

> In case this interloper Salé should be allowed to remain in Rimi, the people will move against him. The Rimi people are too proud to bear the rule of a foreign upstart. Within twenty-four hours, the Rimi people will make war upon this man and his accomplices, and if he remains in Rimi, I forgo all responsibility for the consequences, be what they may (p. 216).

The irony of the document—an irony he obviously did not intend—is that Aladai sees Salé but not Burwash as a 'foreign interloper' whom the 'proud' Rimi people cannot bear to serve. It is unintended, it seems, because nowhere else in the novel is the presence of the British administration questioned in any intrinsic way. On the occasion of this letter, as on a later one when Aladai is up in arms against the government,

87

he is primarily opposing the rule of his rivals. Thus what his 'nationalism' amounts to is his search for a parallel place with the British officials to do 'good' for the Rimis. He is seeking, in other words, to be a black equivalent, in the political sphere, of Albert Schweitzer and Dr Schlemm. Aladai's interview with Mr Burwash over education and his discussions with Judy on the matter (pp. 68–70) offer good instances of this fact. We may say, then, that in *The African Witch*, the radical question of imperial political power, as opposed to the domestic squabbling of rival claimants to the local throne, is not raised.

Cary claims in the Preface that the novel began 'in a sketch . . . of an African nationalist. I called him the Black Prince, and he was, as far as I can remember, a much more violent and hysterical man than Aladai' (p. 9). The point, though, is not that Aladai is not violent or hysterical enough, but that he had no political purpose deserving either violence or hysteria.

> 'Are you a nationalist?' [Judy asked him] cautiously.
> 'I don't know,' he answered; and then, speaking with force, 'I think I am—if that means standing up for one's own people.'
> Judy heard the tremor of excitement in the boy's voice, and remembered his swaggering uneasiness in the race course.
> She was glad to change the subject (p. 21).

What Aladai's nationalism turns out to be is a generous admiration of English and European values. That is to say, his ideal of nationalism is the same as that of the Victorian colonial philanthropists who sought to bring as much as possible of Europe into Africa.

> 'I can't understand it,' he burst out. 'Such a great people—a great civilisation! And they see I love it. Think of how I felt when I began to read English books and to hear what civilisation could mean—it was like growing up thousands of years in a few months' (p. 24).

In the absence of any political commitment on Aladai's part, we do not have a substantial evaluation of whatever conflict may have been implicit in the presence of English officials in Rimi. Later in the novel, Elizabeth and the women organise a resistance movement. But, again, the objective was not to eliminate British authority but to break the religious influence of the missions and the political power of the Muslims. This is not to say that there is no political activity in the novel or that, in Cary's larger sense of the term, there is no political conflict. It is to say that on the political front of the 'war' in *The African Witch*, issues are never joined on the level that would have mattered most. On the one side we see the nature of the British colonial administration as reflected in the conduct of its various agents: the temporising Burwash, the obedient Fisk, the young and arrogant Rackham. On the other side we see the political activity of the Emir and his shambles of an administration. We see the nature of the conflicts which ensue between the Emir, the Muslim Salé and the pagan people. We find three activists—Elizabeth, Aladai, Coker—introducing complications to an already agitated community. In all that confusion, the fact of British presence seems taken for granted, because necessary; accordingly issues are not joined between the possibly anarchical forces of the local people and the order of British power.

There would be little point in stressing these points were it not that Cary's one voice or style which aims at an inclusiveness and subtlety of response is at odds with another which seeks only the definition of point of view and the certainty of graphic symbolism. So insistent is the one style on recapturing the actuality of Rimi life that the effort of the other to simplify that life for the purposes of symbolic presentation becomes, not merely inconsistent, but seriously misleading. This degeneration is to be seen in the development of the character of Aladai and Coker; it is to be seen in the way the characterisation of the principal African characters (e.g. Elizabeth) contrasts with the characterisation of the insignificant ones (e.g. Fanta). But we can see it, most clearly, in the third front of this 'war', the racial front. There, race conflict, as social and moral drama, is placed alongside a view of the same conflict as a theological contest—theological in the sense that instead of one error being pitted against another, one virtue against another, some presumed good is contrasted with an evil, some code of honour with its absence, England with the jungle. The effect is rather predictable, even if often impressive. Thus, for example, the scene at the waterside between Fisk and Aladai, ends with Aladai's protestations of the dignity of England.

> Aladai's voice was also changed, and his manner. He no longer stood stiffly and behaved with a nonchalance which was slightly mocking. His neck bent; his hands went up; his back stooped; his eyes were full of sympathy and affection. There is no other word for their eager response to Fisk's change of tone. He exclaimed, 'Fisk, will you believe I am not your enemy? I am very loyal; perhaps I am more loyal than you yourself. I am a prince—or very little prince— and to me the King of England gives feelings of great tenderness and honour. We in Rimi are only too willing to be his people' (p. 205).

Cary introduces this third front of the 'war' in his native or indigenous style: 'An awkward incident took place at Rimi races' (p. 15). The 'incident' is a racial confrontation, and the key to Cary's attitude to it is in the very word 'awkward' which defines a moral situation in terms of social comedy and deliberately converts the moral urgency of the occasion into a social embarrassment. This conversion does not, however, obliterate the moral implications of the incident, for the point of view of the narration takes both the social fact and its moral implications seriously. That is to say, the point of view allows for the social arrangement which 'in practice . . . excludes all natives except a few magnates like the Emir and his ministers' from the grandstands; but it still judges that arrangement wrong. The gentleman's code which rational- ised the exclusion of Africans from the stand also understood its own 'immorality', and therefore preferred that the rationale for the code should not be questioned. It understood, in other words, that the presence of the black 'intruders'—'two Negroes in European dress'—was 'awkward' in the sense, according to the dictionaries, of being 'dangerous to deal with'. There is thus implicit in the admission of an 'awkward-ness', an awareness of the irrational or immoral character of the exclusion.

Cary does not present this awareness in theological terms; rather he shows the operation of the minds of people wedded to the security of their arrangement. The result is comedy of a most painful sort; especially as the comedy depends on the realisation by all parties of the social and moral embarrass-ments of the actual predicament. Hence the white population finds excuse for their resentment of the Africans in the 'dandified perfection' of one of them, in their 'nonchalance' and 'gaiety', and in the fact that they 'laughed together at the remark made by one of them' (p. 15). The laughter 'infuriated the little white woman [Mrs Pratt],' and she 'wanted to strike the smiling faces—beat them down' (p. 15). The comedy and the painfulness of this incident coincide at the moment when the white population and the reader concede the basic injustice and the bigotry of the social code. It is indicative of the extent to which the two Africans relate themselves to this code that their intrusion is not even a calculated assault on the moral and social situation, but an accidental (though unregretted) breach of it.

> The two Negroes, finding themselves stared at, had lost their self-confidence. They looked uneasily round them—the mulatto with an arrogant glassy stare, the other nervously. But he, too, gave his hat a cock over one eye; struck an arrogant pose.
>
> This enraged the watchers. A voice near Rackham called out—loud enough to be heard by the offenders—'Kick them out'. Two young bankers from the north, and a soldier stood planted opposite them, like dogs about to spring.
>
> Rackham, too, wanted to do something violent—to inflict public humiliation on the pair. He said bitterly, 'Something like this was bound to happen—I told the Resident, but he wouldn't let me put the police on the ropes' (p. 17).

What we have here, then, is social comedy, but it is also (and seriously) moral tragedy. The stage is set for conflict. On the one hand the Africans—arrogant, nervous, cocky; on the other, the whites—also arrogant, nervous and cocky. But

91

actual conflict is impossible because the allegiances which shape these responses are different. It is in the process of explaining and dramatising these different allegiances that Cary moves away from the subtlety of his native style to the diagrammatic convenience of his pseudo-Conradian style. The result is that the tragedy of the racial conflict in the novel now depends on the innate inadequacy of the African element in the character of Aladai and Coker, rather than on the prior existence of an irrational and an immoral code. In other words, the bottom is taken off the social and moral structure established for us in the first chapter. Since this consequence is crucial to the final evaluation of the novel and relevant to an understanding of Cary's fictional method, we will explore Cary's study of this racial conflict in some detail.

Two passages will help pin-point the two approaches to the issue of race which Cary adopts in the novel. In a scene early in the novel, Cary introduces Osi, 'a young girl lately married' who was 'conspicuous by her new clothes'.

> She was like a child in church trying to be serious, but so much excited by the crowd, by her own new cloth, of bright blue plush, wrapped round her firm maiden's breasts, by the glances cast at her, and the sudden importance of her family, that she could not manage to be so for more than half a minute at a time (p. 31).

This account tries to explain Osi's conduct in terms of what might be called the constants of human psychology. Her actions in the situation are thus a response to life itself, to her delight in her own existence.

> Whenever the father spoke, Osi turned up her shining eyes towards him and looked grave; but even before he had finished, she had caught some passing eye, noticed a wrinkle in her cloth, and at once she was preening herself, moving her lips self-consciously, wriggling her shoulders, peeping over her shoulder. Once she smiled at a friend, showing all her brilliant teeth, her childish delight (p. 31).

Behind this delight and perhaps encouraging it is the presence of her husband, 'a powerful young man of eighteen, with an extremely ugly but good-natured face. Ojo was very black, and smallpox had left his skin as rough as old weatherworn rock. One nostril had been partly eaten away.' She never moved from Ojo's 'presence', 'an aura which seemed to extend about six inches from him in every direction. When he moved, she moved, not touching him, but keeping as much of herself as possible within that aura. Even when she was looking another way, she moved with him, as if she could feel his presence like a magnetic charge, whose strength informed her of his distance' (p. 31).

Osi's conduct represents a frank human response. By a simple alteration of the details, the picture could be painted of any other woman in a similar circumstance. Osi, that is, is a human being. Her skin may be the 'colour of milk chocolate', her nose 'broad, smooth, and flat, with perfectly even-flared nostrils', her lips may be 'full and curled, but not turned out', her waist as 'little . . . as the classical Venus'. Her calf may 'come lower than a white woman's' and thus avoid 'the ugly forms of a pegtop'. She may finally, have suffered from smallpox so that she had 'one noticeable depression—in the middle of her left cheek, so placed that it was a beauty spot' (p. 31). Yet her responses to life, however unique, remain human. Such a total human response, as so often in Cary, is its own justification and makes comparisons superfluous. As such, it does not lend itself to the dramatic violence of treatment which, Cary claimed, he needed for an African novel.

In the second passage, on the other hand, Cary records the same totality of response, but explains it, no longer in terms of personality but in terms of a mystique of race. Akande Tom was understandably delighted with his suit of clothes; 'had it been rags, so long as they were European rags, it would have given Tom an indescribable happiness'. Cary did not mean this explanation to be limited to Tom and his kind of man, but to be applied to all Africans.

> For the difference, even in a snob's imagination, between a peer and
> a tramp is nothing to that in a savage's between himself and a white
> man. It is so great that the bush Negro does not concern himself
> with it. His indifference to the white man and his ideas is founded on

a feeling of difference so profound that his mind will not attempt to pass over the gap. Only the most enterprising, like Tom—men of ambition and ideals—attempt it (p. 148–149).

Accordingly, in his white rags, Tom 'felt as near a white man as it was possible for him to be, and enjoyed *an exaltation which might possibly be compared with that of a risen soul on his first morning in paradise*' (italics added). The contrast with Osi's exaltation is only too obvious. Osi is in her world, in spite of her 'clothes'. Her stability, her capacity to absorb the clothes without being overwhelmed by the fact that it is a 'white' phenomenon, contrasts with Tom's supposed commitment to the idea of white 'being and power' (p. 149). This contrast is significant, in another sense. Osi's response—which in its own way is a virtue—does not stand in the context of the race-conflict of *The African Witch* as a positive, only as a neutral fact, whereas Tom's 'disease' is made into a virtue—that of the ambitious and the idealistic.

This paradox of values is not difficult to explain. The norms which are used to present the African world in the novel are precisely those which attach a virtue to any aspiration to or enthusiastic worship of the European ideal. Hence the stupidity of Tom's 'thinking' is made into an African or a savage virtue arising, it is suggested, from an African emotionalism. 'Akande's reasoning was not logical or definitive. It was part of his feelings. The whole process was one of thought-feeling carried on by every part of his nervous system, from the ends of his crinkled hair to the tips of his long, thick-jointed toes' (p. 149).

We are not arguing here that such a conclusion is not possible and legitimate, or that Cary should not have alluded to it. We only want to draw attention to the fact that Cary is stating such a conclusion and that, taken along with Cary's other voice which states otherwise, the finality of that conclusion not only becomes untenable in itself but contradicts the general assumption of that other point of view. That finality is, in fact, questioned even in this scene when, reverting to his indigenous mode, Cary shows Musa, leader of the group of 'ten or a dozen idle carriers and small boys' parodying Tom's presumption. Musa and his friends were

> ... walking in front of Tom with a peculiar toe and heel movement, like a white man in boots, peering, with thumbs and fingers for goggles, to right and left and shouting, 'I am the big judge Akande Tom, brother of the Sultan of England, not very distantly related to the cannon ju-ju and closely connected with the backside of the camel' (p. 149).

The effect of this *reductio ad absurdum* ought to have been to expose the obtuseness of Tom's aspirations. Musa, ridiculing Tom and his mystique of a white suit, should have served, as similar juxtapositions do in *An American Visitor*, to bring the generalisation into question. That it does not, that Cary does not make it do so, is indicative of the strength of the generalisation as a convenient and even reassuring faith, and of the difficulties inherent in Cary's use of that faith in his treatment of racial conflict in the novel.

In the opening scene of the novel, Cary does not invoke this faith. The behaviour of Coker and Aladai in appearing at the stands is not ascribed to any over-riding African (i.e. 'savage') disposition; similarly, Mrs Pratt's fury at their non-chalance and gaiety is the 'natural' result of her social and racial situation, not of any Saxon or white temperament, from which it is impossible for her to escape. There is nothing in her being English which makes it inevitable that she should behave in that way; there is, however, everything in her psychological situation as a white woman among Africans, to make her response not only necessary but proper. But the opening scene, as we saw, only prepared the ground for a conflict; it did not present the conflict itself. By following the development of this conflict especially as it relates to Aladai, we can show how the psychological foundation on which the opening scene was based gives way to the stereotypical faith on which Tom's characterisation had depended.

Two illustrative examples of this shift will be cited here in order, particularly, to demonstrate that the question at issue is a critical not a sociological one. According to Harry Barba, 'in the earliest pages of the novel, Aladai defies the white man's conventions by doing two things: he enters the restricted pavilion at the race track and barges in on an exclusive bonfire club. But, more than that, he stays on in spite of painful snubs.'[1] This interpretation accords with the impression which the opening chapter gives, that Aladai is a conscious revolutionary, confident and purposive. The fact is, however, that as Aladai is developed in the novel, he is far from possessing any qualities of conscious purposiveness or confidence. First, he does not 'defy the white man's conventions' by entering the restricted zone. When he discusses the incident with Judy, Aladai makes it clear that he intended no defiance.

> He turned suddenly towards her and said, 'Ought I to have gone into the enclosure?'
>
> 'It didn't matter a bit—but I believe one is supposed to have an invitation.'
>
> 'Coker said that I wouldn't need one, as a Rimi prince.'
>
> 'Perhaps you don't. I'm sure you wouldn't. No, of course, not. I'm sure if you ask the Resident——'
>
> 'But people thought I was pushing myself in——'
>
> 'They didn't understand that you had a right to be there.'
>
> The young man walked up and down with quick nervous steps, then, unexpectedly, he smiled at his friend, and said, 'If I had put on a turban, and three or four Hausa gowns, they'd have been delighted to see me. . . . Why do they not like me to wear their clothes—isn't it a compliment?' (p. 23).

Judy is the subtler of the two, having been able to evade admitting what she knew to be the irrational and violent nature of the European attitude to the 'cannibal prince'. Aladai, for his part is singularly incapable of addressing himself to the radical question of race-prejudice, in imagining, as he does here, that that prejudice is the expression of the proverbial English refusal of a compliment! Aladai, then, is not defying any convention: 'Coker said that I wouldn't need [an invitation] as a Rimi prince.'

[1] Harry Barba, 'Cary's Image of the African in Transition', *University of Kansas Review*, XXIX (Summer, 1963), p. 291.

Nor does he 'barge in on the exclusive bonfire club'. As the novel explains, Aladai 'had not fully understood that he was making history, but he was also alarmed. The fear and the delight were, as usual, there together, maintaining each other' (pp. 114–115). What had happened to him at the club takes on a different meaning in the light of this authorial explanation. When Aladai saw that the Resident was absent 'he felt panic. He had counted on the Resident. . . . He had not realised till now how much he had dared by this expedition, how much his longing for the company of white people had influenced him to risk it and how much he had depended on the Resident. He was for the moment blind with panic' (p. 115). He did not run off the scene only because he was 'with his own servants, and under the eyes of townspeople. He could not turn back and acknowledge to them, "I am a conceited fool, and not even a brave one." He could not have made his muscles and his nerves accept such a humiliation; for they were prouder than his mind' (p. 115).

These two illustrations serve one purpose. They show that if one assumes whatever weaknesses are detected in Aladai's character as in fact his native strength, one sees his actual strengths as derived solely from his contact with Europe. If, on the other hand, one assumes that his weaknesses are his, in a personal and not a racial sense, then neither these weaknesses nor his strengths can be so easily attributed to either his European or his African personalities. In an interesting meeting between him and Burwash, Aladai is shown as having been taken in by Burwash's polite, diplomatic but sarcastic manner. Judy saw that Burwash was making fun of Aladai, and said as much to Aladai. '"Don't be too hopeful, Louis. You heard what Mr Burwash said— 'slow and sure'. . . . Well, he was friendly, but——"' (p. 70). But Oxford-educated and civilised Aladai cannot detect this. When he left Burwash's office, he 'walked out backwards; or, if not exactly backwards, sideways. "Thank you awfully, sir, You are truly, in the words of my own country, 'a father and a mother'"' (p. 70). He tells Judy, 'I felt like going down on my nose to him.'

> Do you know I was not conscious of being obsequious at all. I simply felt love for him, real love. You think that is sentimental. . . . Emotional, then. It is a Rimi fault, we show our feelings too much and especially our affectionate feelings (p. 70).

One can visualise a man such as Aladai, but one will see his behaviour, in this case, as his personal failing, not as his racial virtue, or a 'Rimi fault'. What discredits the insight of Cary's view of the race-conflict in *The African Witch* is his attempt to present all the personal failings in Aladai's character as the actual strengths of his racial temperament.

This conclusion is not so far-fetched as it might seem. Harry Barba, for example, begins his study of Cary's African-in-transition with an endorsement of Harold R. Collins' opinion that 'far from being eternally backward, far from being "India rubber idiots on a spree," [Cary's Africans] adopt European ideas and ways, often with maddening inconsistency, unexpected lapses, and shocking backsliding.'[1] Though endorsing this view as 'apt', Barba insists, however, on distinguishing between Aladai, whom he calls 'a civilised city man' and characters like Uli and Obai, who are '"stone age" natives'. What he means by this distinction is that whereas Uli and Obai are 'eternally backward' 'idiots on a spree', Aladai, 'true to his Oxford education', is 'civilised'.

Having taken these positions—which are legitimate, given the terms of Cary's novel—Barba goes on to explain Aladai's failures in terms of an inexorable racial characteristic. The 'urges of primordial blood', he says, 'are strong, too, though quiescent; for, in spite of his European education, he is still a Nigerian at heart, a child of the African wilds'.[2] 'At times [Aladai] shows both his native cunning and the special opportunism of any European demagogue'; and 'also in

---

[1] Harry Barba, op. cit., p. 291. Collins' remark appeared in 'Joyce Cary's Troublesome Africans', *Antioch Review*, XIII (1953), p. 406.
[2] Barba, op. cit., p. 291.

keeping with his Nigerian roots, Aladai is very emotional when shown a kindness'. To support this last statement, Barba quite legitimately quotes Aladai's own words, already cited, that he felt like going down on his nose to Burwash. 'Like Uli, Aladai shows a response to the call of blood which is stronger than the influence of his contact with civilisation.'[1] Uli's fate, he argues, was not tragic, because he had 'no real choice . . . since there was really no opportunity to do other than he did—whereas Aladai's tragedy is that he knew there was something immensely more desirable (which he learned about and experienced at Oxford)'.[2] In conclusion, Barba characterises Aladai's tragedy as 'a triumph for the primordial, retrogressive urges that dominate the Nigerian. . . . The Black Prince is killed and his sister, the African Witch, triumphs.'[3]

The vastness and the finality of these generalisations about 'the Nigerian mind' sound more inexcusable than they really are; for they are indeed justified by the rhetoric of the novel itself. What needs to be questioned, therefore, is not the criticism which so naïvely fails to call the rhetoric to question, but the fiction which employs it. In a dramatisation of the triumph of primordial urges over civilisation, the conflicts in Aladai which Cary posits may indeed be pertinent, but not the use of such conflicts as a means of understanding either the individual hero or the race. The central weakness of Cary's treatment of race in *The African Witch* and of the character of Aladai is this—that because Cary sees in all of Aladai's personal weaknesses evidence of his racial heritage, the subsequent war between white and black is really one between God and a straw man.

Aladai, we are told, is full of excitement of an animal kind. In his very first meeting with Judy, he passed 'in an instant . . . from one kind of excitement to another, equally exuberant' (p. 25). Judy is afraid that 'the young man was again growing too enthusiastic' (p. 25). In his meeting with Burwash he 'unconsciously . . . bent forward smiling; his eyes

[1] Ibid., p. 292.   [2] Ibid., p. 292.   [3] Ibid., p. 292.

turned slightly upward'. In response, Burwash 'smiled *upon* him' (p. 69). So honoured is he to be received by the Resident that, as he talked it over with Judy, she 'feared that some of the emotion in his voice might appear in his too expressive features, and that her look would increase it' (p. 70). On being introduced to Mrs Vowls ('who plainly took little stock of the graces of life whether in dress or manner', and who Judy feared 'would insult her friend'), Aladai 'with a most wretched air performed a third lower bow, almost a cringe' (p. 71). She, for her part 'smiled not merely graciously but even tenderly' (p. 71). In his first direct encounter with Rackham, he cannot see through the white man's irony as they talk about black skies.

> 'Is that why it's blacker some nights?'
> Aladai answered at once: 'So I believe. When the upper air is quite clear of vapour, or more than usually clear.'
> His voice shook a little. He sat forward in his chair, leaning towards Rackham with an eager politeness. His voice was eloquent of his grateful feelings (p. 116).

The brilliance of this comedy appertains to more than Aladai's personal obtuseness and is assumed as a natural part of Aladai's sensationalist heritage, as a fact of his tribal mentality.[1] As a result, Aladai is almost forgiven his mediocrity because of his race. Thus, also, the comic humour of Aladai's meeting with Dryas becomes, by the very terms of Cary's racial generalisations in the novel, a miniature version of the encounter of the races. Dryas, 'obeying a routine of a week', had turned towards the club chairs and walked into the circle when she noticed Aladai's presence. 'Then obviously she received a shock' (p.121). Aladai saw her turn away. 'For a moment, Aladai was hovering in the air, with one hand on his chair, half up and half down, while the girl stood on one foot, like a stork' (p. 121). When, like the 'young lady of the finishing school', she recovered herself and shook

[1] Harold C. Collins (op. cit., p. 404) believes this of Africans. 'Well, Africans usually do appear childish in white men's novels. Indeed Africans seem so to most white observers, and it is natural that they should.'

hands with him, Aladai 'in his sudden leap of anxious polite-
ness, nearly butted her in the face' (p. 121). 'After a little
thought [she] made some remark', and Aladai answered
'with his most Continental gestures. He looked at one moment as if he was going to fall on his knees beside her and put
his head in her lap' (p. 122).

That this comedy is intended as part of the war between
cultures and races, we can deduce from other incidents. In
the opening scene, for example, Cary had associated the
African's 'emotionalism' to his innate sense of inferiority, and
had symbolised this in the relationship between Judy and
Aladai. Hence, in speaking of the fact that Aladai was a
prince, Judy 'confined herself to exclamations because she
knew that her young friend was still agitated. He was breathing fast, and a light sweat glistened on his high black fore-
head and pointed cheeks. His swaggering walk—all his
movements were still exaggerated. He was in the condition
of a nervous boy who has just passed through a critical test'
(p. 19). As she leaves the stadium, with Aladai and Coker on
each side of her, they leaned 'inwards as if attracted by the
powerful influence of her race and sex' (p. 18). This 'powerful influence of her race and sex' determines Aladai's response
to her. As he led her towards Elizabeth's shrine, for instance,
his nerves were still

> quivering with the excitement of a princely ovation and a woman's
> homage. In England, Judy's friendship had meant little to him.
> Prettier and more distinguished women had received him. But in
> Africa already, as if the political atmosphere were a real aerial
> fluid affecting its inhabitants by mere absorption, he felt towards
> her the respect, gratitude, and admiring affection due to a princess
> by one whom she has deeply obliged (p. 38).

He gladly agrees to enter the town from which he was
barred because 'he could not bear to deprive himself of the
pleasure of continuing in Judy's company' (pp. 38–39).

It is important to note that Cary writes only of Aladai's
'pleasure in the company' of Judy, as in the company of
Dryas, since the connection between them is so compromised

101

by the presumptions of the novel's dialectic that it becomes mere indulgence to speak of the 'affair' between these girls and Aladai. The novel explains the nature of their relationship. If Aladai had been white, Judy

> would not have been so much impressed by his intelligence. . . . But even if he had been white, she would have been delighted by his quick sympathy, his instant response to shades of meaning and feeling. She found in him the real capacity for friendship, which is sympathy of mind—as sympathy of heart is that of love (p. 20).

Aladai's response to her and to Dryas is determined less by the 'sympathy of the heart' than by the power of whiteness. This fact is made quite clear in Aladai's connection with Dryas. In her company, he was 'so happy that he could not help making a noise. He shouted at his servants to express the elation of his spirits and feeling . . . he was in love, and he thought that he had made an impression on her.' But:

> He did not suppose that this girl loved him, any more than he would have expected love from an angel.
>
> This feeling of the loved one's angelic separateness may belong to any Englishman, but not in the same degree, for, though angels may exist for them as ideas, potent and real as Britannia or La France in action, they aren't to be met with in flesh and blood— creatures of a different colour and beauty from one's own mortal race (pp. 167–168).

This generalisation naturally conditions our interpretation of two other incidents involving Dryas and Aladai. One is his letter to her expressing his 'gratitude for an action of kindness, to use a very inadequate word, which was so spontaneous and magnanimous that it surpassed my belief in human nature; I almost put here my belief in white human nature' (p. 125). Dryas's 'action of kindness', it turns out, was in enduring their brief encounter at the bonfire club. 'If I could be honoured to die for you, I should yet be satisfied . . . it is not easy to defy the scorn and hatred of one's friends, and for what, to succour an impudent Negro' (p. 121).

The other incident follows the entertainment which Aladai provided for Dryas during their abortive trip to Schlemm's mission when they had tried to dance. What she 'disliked' was his 'hand touching her back, but again she suppressed her distaste'. Faithful to his emotionalism and his belief in goodness, he does not notice. 'I need not tell you what happiness you have given me—what great happiness—and—confidence. I think I owe very much to you—I must not say what I feel' (p. 169). If Dryas is to Aladai an angel-in-the-flesh, and if it is to be understood that this is so because Dryas represents whiteness, then the scene does not so much make Aladai a fool as it makes him an African. That is to say that Aladai is not being a fool because he is a fool, but because he is an African: 'Though Aladai had the subtlety of Hamitic blood in him, he was not subtle enough to know that the compliment [of merely turning her eyes 'towards the man's face'] was not so much for him as for his disabilities' (p. 166).

If this is the truth (and the novel's symbolism assumes this), then the racial bigotry of the white population, though in bad taste, is a natural and civilised response to the racial inadequacies of black humanity. Or ought to be. But Cary's interest in race prejudice as irrational and unjustified forces him to make Aladai the superior intellectual he is not, and cannot be.

> When Honeywood called Aladai a performing ape, or a monkeyfied Bolshie, he was using Rackham's own words. But Rackham knew perfectly well that Aladai was worth six Honeywoods, both as a man and an intelligence; he was worth an infinity of Honeywoods, because Honeywood was a robot, a set of reactions, a creature ruled entirely by prejudice and a mass of contradictory impulses and inhibitions, which he called his opinions, and thought of as his character. He was a wooden man danced on strings; and anyone could make him kick. The word Bolshie, for instance, caused one reaction—not a mental, but a nervous, reaction—and the word nigger caused another.
>
> His brain did not seek to judge and know; it existed to scheme defence and satisfaction for the beasts and parasites lodged in the zoo of his character. . . .
>
> To Rackham, people like Honeywood were more disgusting than to a tolerant and patient Englishman, for he loathed his stupidity. He was a dull fungus. He had not even colour or interest as a curiosity (pp. 192–193).

The comparison is pointed, but hopelessly inadequate as a correction in emphasis. It does not, for example, correct Mr. Father's prejudice provoked by the same robot-like attitude as Honeywood's. '"What good," he asked, "is P. G. Wodehouse to these——". He swallowed the word in deference to the lady. He was polite' (p. 264). The fact is that given the novel's argument, Wodehouse can do little good. Aladai's Oxford education only produced the Wordsworth-quoting bore of the bonfire episode, and deserved Rackham's mutter, 'Oh Gawd' (p. 117). And even if Aladai is 'superior' to Honeywood, is he equal, much less superior, to Rackham? Even if he is, how does one rank Aladai's countrymen with the European bankers and officials?

The fact is, clearly, that one set of terms which Cary uses in this novel to characterise race conflict is in opposition to another set of assumptions about human action on which most of the novel depends. The assumption that Elizabeth's ju-ju and Coker's emotionalism are symbolic of the African personality compromises any attempt to insist on the integrity or respectability of that personality whenever it is in conflict with an alien character. Thus while one Carian voice claims that Dryas was 'particularly polite' to Aladai, 'not only because she felt a nervous disgust of his black skin' but also because 'she sympathised with him for being black' (p. 165), that she 'saw that she was making him happy—making him forget his inferiority' (p. 166),[1] the other voice argues that Aladai was equal, even superior, to the Europeans and that Dryas's attitude ought to have been different. Similarly, one voice endorses Judy's rejection of local snobbery against Aladai, while another allows that, in her proper mood, she herself would have behaved like the others. In arguing against Honeywood's bigotry, Judy had reminded him that he had danced with 'one of the Blackbird girls'.

[1] Cf. *Aissa Saved* (Carfax ed. 1952), p. 44 where Mrs Carr is 'disgusted' by Musa's 'anxious civility to the white people even more than his abuse of the mob.'

'Well, that was—well—in London—after all.' Honeywood was taken aback.

'What's the difference?'

'All the difference?'

'All the difference,' said Rackham briefly, coming to the rescue (p. 197).

As if to assent to Rackham's distinction, Judy, 'who knew there was a difference, shifted her ground. "I don't believe it anyhow. And I'm sure [Aladai] treated Dryas like a princess. I knew him pretty well. . . . He thinks she's a kind of angel. . . . He's most frightfully anxious to do the right thing and to be appreciated"' (p. 197).

In order to do the 'right thing and to be appreciated', Aladai had to be English (or European). He had to transcend the limitations of racial ('primordial') encumbrances and attain a harmony of personality capable of sustaining 'civilisation' and avoiding 'barbarism'. This is Aladai's task, as Cary sees it, and his failure to accomplish it is, ultimately, the only explanation of his tragedy, as the final movements of the novel testify. There Cary attempts to explain Aladai's failure in terms of the contrary tendencies of his African and his European personalities. This contradiction of tendencies, expressed as a conflict within Aladai himself, is the fourth 'front' of the war in *The African Witch*, and is easily documented.

We have already pointed out the 'native psychology' which Aladai is made to represent, and the extent to which Cary goes to emphasise its pertinence to Aladai's conduct. 'All of Louis' civilised instincts', Andrew Wright states, 'are revolted by [Coker]; and yet, near the end of the book when Coker has made a sacrifice of the Schweitzer-like Dr Schlemm and has put his head on display, Louis feels the power and the temptation of this emphasis in religion.'[1] Wright's tone is more casual than is necessary. For the final phase of Aladai's career is unquestionably governed by the contradictory pressures of his assumed primitive African and

---

[1] *Joyce Cary*, p. 81.

his civilised European propensities. In this final phase, the subtle and oblique manner in which this view has been expressed yields to the overt contrasts which Wright was probably thinking of in his summation and which Harry Barba emphasised in his.

There is ground for their views. After the bush-party with Dryas, Aladai looked out to a view which was 'at the same time a challenge and a delight'. Through his African temperament, the 'wildness' of the scene 'entered into the exhilaration which made him feel that he too, like the boat-man, would like to drink, sing, dance all night, to perform astonishing feats of rejoicing' (p. 170). The other tempera-ment in him—the European—made other claims. The scene 'challenged the Englishman in him, who wanted to build' (p. 170). The simplicity of this opposition is not accidental. At the riverside scuffle,

> Aladai turned round, became an English gentleman, and advanced with a solicitous air. . . . Aladai whipped [the hat] off again, brushed it with his sleeve, replaced it the right way round.
> 'I'm most frightfully sorry, sir.' He began to bow, but recollected himself (p. 203).

Later in the same scene he protests his allegiance to Fisk. '"I am very loyal [to England]; perhaps I am more loyal than you yourself. I am a prince—a very little prince, I know, but still a prince—and to me the King of England gives feelings of great tenderness and honour. We in Rimi are only willing to be his people"' (p. 205). Nor is that all. 'As Aladai gave rein to his feelings [his African quality], he was carried into Rimi thought and his English suffered' (p. 205). Similarly, in rejecting Dr Schlemm's advice against a war on Salé's faction, Aladai, for all the formality of a native garb, was a divided man: 'in spite of his dress', he 'was easy and non-chalant, already the European' (p. 215).

What fortifies this consistent, if mechanical, explanation of Aladai's personality is the notion, beautifully presented in a river-scene between Aladai and Judy, that the African 'demon' is a jealous god, a god of blood; and that consequently every manifestation of the African mind would tend toward the death-bringing and the irrational. In the river scene, Aladai and his singers retell how an old mother sacrificed herself to the river god, in order to end a famine.

'*She threw herself into the black water.*
The river accepted the old woman.'

Then, quickening again to a dance rhythm (they sang):

'*The black water is joyful with her blood.*
It runs and leaps. It is dark and thick.
The great fish moves its tail and swims in the thick water.
He is not angry. His people remember him' (pp. 160–161).

Judy is puzzled by the implications of the song, and asks Aladai why a 'father' should 'want a sacrifice'. '"I suppose he is a jealous god," said Aladai.'

Aladai believed himself to be an inheritor of this religion of blood. In the final scenes of the novel, when the people, led by Coker, clamour for general death, Aladai sees in it a manifestation of African genius.

'We must all die,' moaned Aladai. 'He that is first—must be the sacrifice. It is very odd, all this,' said the brain, in a European voice. 'I shall speak to Miss Judy about this. Why this lust for death. It does not seem natural. Nature wants to live—not to die. Why should the beast blood want to pour itself out?

Why does the blood love pain as well as joy? What is this spite and jealousy in flesh? Why do people cut themselves for the *ju-ju*? What is the god of nature—this reasoning of blood soaked for a million years in the agony of beasts? . . . At each shout, Aladai swayed, jerked, wobbled; his moans were cries of pain, and he, too, moved towards the swamp. He did not know what he wanted, but his body moved towards the swamp. It was wet with fear. . . .

'But what nonsense,' said the brain briskly, like a tutor, but less polite. 'That won't do Rimi any good—What Rimi wants is peace, trade—schools——'

'Rimi,' he moaned. 'Rimi, my country—I give my life—for the love of Rimi.'

'Rimi,' said the brain, 'is a *ju-ju* for the herd—the religion of the blood, the race, the old crocodile——'

'Rimi,' he shrieked. 'For Rimi——' (pp. 292–293).

This conflict within Aladai is of course a conflict also between the races, between the tutor (the brain) and the beast (the body). The body he acquired by his race; his brain was his inheritance by his English education. It is no surprise that when Rackham and Judy interrupt the scene, Aladai finds their presence his one hope for peace of mind. Somebody calls out: '"Aladai, the white woman,"' and the words 'brought such relief and comfort as he had not known since he had first swayed in the ju-ju crowd; it was as if he once more found himself *among his own kind, but this time English people*, sensible people' (p. 294; italics added). He may have had thoughts of putting Rackham to death. 'But just now he was English. He was even dressed as an Englishman . . . Aladai walked up to Rackham, and offered his hand. Rackham hesitated for a moment, and then shook the hand' (p. 295). But for all his share of English common sense, Aladai remains the African. Judy tried till she was exhausted to argue him out of the madness of a rising against Salé. 'She knew that she was dealing with one of those obsessions which seize upon every brain at times, but especially the half-educated, and the Negroes; and she fought it with the only weapon she had—sense, ridicule, abuse' (p. 196). Because he would not listen to the last desperate voice of Europe, Aladai engages in his abortive campaign and dies shouting 'something' about Rimi. 'No one could distinguish what it was' (p. 298).

What the novel affirms, then, is its own assumptions, the power of a base African nature over the higher European intellect; the tragedy of Africa as the tragedy of its own nature. Aladai and (on a smaller scale) Tom thus become the human equivalents of the continental struggle between intellect and passion, civilisation and barbarism. When Tom, who tried to imitate the white man, was finally humiliated by his frenzied countrymen, he was only left with his African body which now seemed to be 'spreading like a flattened boneless mass—a black jelly, protoplasm' (p. 208). What the witchcraft of Africa had done to him was to make him revert to the manner of a beast, 'like a baboon, shuffling to and fro, stooping down; and his meaningless speech was like monkey chatter'. Africa 'stared, fascinated, to see the witch's work on the man; to watch him change from man to beast, with a beast's stupid brain' (p. 307).

In the final analysis, then, the 'bitter war' which Cary speaks of in his Preface is a managed war. Each party to the war, according to Cary, 'is trying to persuade the other (as well as himself) that his creed is the only reasonable certain truth, and that outside it there is in fact nothing but darkness and devils' (p. 10). As we have shown, the novel itself is contending that outside Christianity and Europe, all else is darkness and devils. The central flaw in Aladai's character, for example, is its native tendency towards this darkness and towards the devil. 'The victory' of traditional Africa at the end of the war, as is only too evident, is also a victory for the devil and for darkness. The natives who torment and ridicule Akande at the end of the novel do so, we are told, 'not only because he tried to escape from the herd, but because they were sunk in fear themselves; and also because some fragment of spirit in them, which knew freedom and had pride, was enslaved inside them, blind and helpless, and forced to eat humiliation every day' (p. 307).

Aladai shares in this enslavement, not in a personal but in a racial sense; that is to say that the possibility of escape from it is virtually non-existent. As Bloom observes; 'Africa is too much for everyone in the novel to grasp or control. [It is] a world where confusion constantly proliferates and people, no matter how dedicated, or gifted, or assertive, constantly fail to master more than a few rudimentary subjective ideas.'[1] The confusion in the execution of the novel's theme is inherent in the very determinism of the novel's world-view. Bloom calls Aladai 'a gifted young idealist eager to bring the blessings of European learning and art to his enslaved people.[2] In the early conversation between Judy and Aladai, Cary

[1] *The Indeterminate World*, p. 54.
[2] Ibid., p. 54.

suggests that this is a task Aladai might yet be able to undertake. But, as the novel itself suggests, not only is Aladai personally incapable of undertaking this task, he could not have undertaken it, even if he had been a different kind of person. Africa is too much for anyone.

It is this unexamined assumption, in fact, which disturbs the novel's argument and therefore forces one to distinguish between the seriousness of the novel's theme, and the solemnity of Cary's execution of it. This is to say that because the novel presumes a tragic environment in Africa which will make a satisfactory accommodation of Africa and Europe impossible, because it does not see that, even so, such an environment would have to be explained in terms of the limitations of particular characters and particular circumstances, the novel fails both to establish the inevitability of the conclusion and to ascertain the dimensions of the disorder which that environment precipitates. The tragic conclusion of *An American Visitor*, as we saw, was related to the conflict between the attempts of a gallery of different persons, black and white, to create institutions for themselves to fulfil their ideal of the good life. Because the continent was long 'preserved' (as Cary saw it) from a great deal of the tumult which accompanies such attempts, the violence and destruction which result are, predictably, more pronounced. Even so, the conflict between the prospectors and Obai was at bottom not a contest between ideal civilisation and brutish barbarism, but between one ideal of material progress and another of traditional local stability. The wisdom of that novel lay in its appreciation both of the tragedy which follows the disappointment of either ideal, and of the character of man himself as the source of and consolation in such tragedy.

In *The African Witch*, however, Cary tries to enforce a deterministic view of the conflict without contending with this earlier wisdom. This suspended circumspection, we have suggested, is the Conradian element in *The African Witch*, and the source of the novel's intellectual weakness. When Dryas and Rackham took their walk, after the parting dinner, to the top of the station hill, the novel tells us that from that height 'the Niger appeared like a sickle-shaped cut in the solid black of the ground backing on the concave slope of Rimi hill' (p. 251). The descriptions that follow, and their overtones of disgust are meant to reflect the mental attitude of the two people, especially that of Dryas:

> In the town a drum began to tap—then two more—out of time. She heard now the murmur of a great many people like wind in grass. Thirty thousand people, the whole dark earth was full of creeping, murmuring. The speck of dirt was crawling with life (p. 252).

In an earlier scene, at Duchi, Dryas had also responded to an African scene. On that occasion, Cary presented two voices—one representing the scene as she saw it, and the other appraising her interpretation of it:

> The sun had just gone down; it, too, threw up a dome of yellow light, steadier and paler than the boatmen's fire, but of the same shape, fading quickly, like the fire, into a greenish halo, and then into the blue-black of a sky more luminous than the burnt earth, but strangely like it in colour. . . .
>
> Dryas stood staring for some minutes, smiling in the proper enjoyment of a view. But her smile disappeared. She was a sincere young woman. She did not know why she felt troubled and inadequate, as if, after all, she did not know what to think of this view. She did not pretend that she was liking it but she continued to look at it. It was after all, a view—sunset in Africa. She must not slight it—(p. 167).

Here Cary's method probes the relationship of the scene, as objective fact, to the person of the viewer. As a result, though there is a close connection between the landscape and Dryas' reaction, this reaction is not mistaken for an inevitable and permanent characteristic of the landscape; more accurately, it is recognised for what it is, the product of a specific observer in a specific state of mind. Cary loses nothing in the process; indeed, he gains a great deal in subtlety, for he allows the reader's critical intelligence to

111

play on Dryas, on the sunset, and on the relationship between the two.

In the later scene in which Dryas and Rackham listen to the drums, Cary makes a leap; and, in his search for graphic certainty, fails to differentiate between the interpretation which Dryas places on the drums, and the construction which the novel itself places on them. Since Dryas' view is a conditioned one—conditioned by what we must assume to be her personal disposition—the coincidence of what she feels with what the novel states becomes both flippant and incongruous. Thus, in the normative voice of the narrator, we are told that 'a fourth drum, a big one, louder, deeper, rumbled with a steady beat. . . . This drum and its heavy shaking beat at once gave centre and measure to all the other sounds—the deep, urgent murmur of voices, the erratic tapping of the smaller drums, a sudden shout of laughter from the barracks, and even the distant yowl of a hyena on the other side of the hill' (p. 252). But also, an interpreting voice seemed to endorse Dryas' view by attaching to the drums and to the scene a significance not attributable to the mentality of any other character.

> It was like a heart beating through the murmur of blood; the working of a body; the amusement and sharp, unexpected pain of a living creature; and now it seemed to be frightened. It was a stupid savage heart, like that of a beast (p. 252).

The coincidence of Dryas' and the novelist's voices is incongruous because in the next few lines the novel casts serious doubts on Dryas' goodwill: her ideal view 'was the English meadows, with well-timbered hedges; or sometimes . . . an Irish landscape with little crooked fields and wide banks' (p. 252). By endorsing a view which coincides with Dryas', the novel thus appropriates to itself a limited viewpoint which it had, ostensibly, rejected. It is a flippant endorsement because if we accept it, the finality of the interpretation becomes a contradiction of the reservations which the novel itself would like to make. The author, that is, gives

112

assent to a conclusion which he does not himself insist on defending.

When we say, therefore, that the novel fails either to establish the inevitability of its conclusion or to ascertain the dimensions of the disorder which its deterministic symbolism presupposes, we are, in effect, saying two things. One is that the novel has not established the relative roles which character and environment play in the tragic action of the novel. The other is that the novel does not show by what logic the tragic world of Elizabeth and Africa sustain its savage kind of order.

'What makes men tick and keeps them ticking?' Cary asks this question in the Preface and claims that whatever the answer, 'you are already deep, whether you like it or not, in metaphysics, in the science of the soul' (pp. 9–10). To answer that question, Cary would have had to measure the dimensions of social and moral order as thoroughly in that novel as he was to do in *To Be a Pilgrim*, in *Charley Is My Darling*, and so extensively in his Second Trilogy. *The African Witch* is, in this light, the most un-Carian of his African novels. A powerful novel in every other respect, *The African Witch* is nevertheless, from this point of view, Cary's most unphilosophical novel, his *Light in August* and his *Victory*.

5: *Tragic and Absurd*

Conrad constantly intrudes into discussions of the character of Joyce Cary's African novels. This is so not only because of the setting of these novels in Africa and of the temperamental affinity between the two novelists but also because of the burden of imperial responsibility which their European heroes have to bear in their encounter with the exotic world of Africa and the Orient: the burden of re-education and self-discovery.

There is a most telling scene at the end of *An American Visitor* which illustrates this point. When Bewsher fell at the hands of the Birri, he had known of this possibility all along and was, in that sense, prepared for it. Dobson, the missionary enthusiast, was incapable of that knowledge and resignation. 'The veriest savage', he preached, 'hesitates to kill the man who comes unarmed and in the name of friendship.'[1] When death comes to Bewsher, however, it is by the hand of his good friend, Obai: 'He [Obai] stood up, opened his chest as if to say, "shoot", and then repeating clearly and proudly his national cry, made a single leap forward and stabbed Bewsher in the chest.'[2]

In many ways, Bewsher's death was unnecessary and irresponsible. As the novel itself says with typical Carian casualness, he 'fell on his back with a look of ludicrous amazement and indignation. . . . In fact, Bewsher's own feelings as he lay on the ground with two or three spears on his body, though of course, full of official indignation, was not empty of a kind of amusement as if some part of his mind were remarking to him, "Well, old chap, the joke is on you.

[1] *An American Visitor*, p. 219.   [2] Ibid., p. 229.

You're not going to get away with it this time"'.[1] The wry humour of this passage would be alien to Conrad's pen; but the self-discovery is totally in his manner. *An American Visitor* is, in that sense, about the education of this white man, just as it is about the education of the primitivist, Miss Hasluck. Accordingly, Cary has to underline the seriousness of this fact while at the same time demonstrating the absence of growth or self-discovery in the Kurtz of his story, Mr Cottee.

Cary's way of doing this is a brilliant passage of interior monologue which dramatises the distance between Cottee's heart and his head, his tragic rejection of romantic heroism.

> Marie's voice had lost some of its quality. It was hoarse and rough. . . . But it had still that power to move, common enough among those who speak with conviction, but always surprising in the force and suddenness of its effects; the power that fills a penitent's bench, that makes an audience of city men stuffed with dinner rise from their seats and shout. It made Cottee's heart beat and his eyes fill. It transported him once more into another state of being, where men and women were born to heroic destinies, and life was the magnificent stage of their glories and their suffering; and it seemed to him, moreover, that the men and women who lived in this other romantic world, call them sentimentalists if you like, were the only ones who knew how to live at all. The rest were the cowards, like himself, who were afraid to love, who were afraid of being laughed at; who mutilated and tamed within themselves every wild creature of the spirit in order to be in safe and comfortable possession of their own farmyard and on good terms with their neighbours. . . .
>
> He half turned towards [Marie], gazed sharply and curiously at the small white face, the big sensitive lips made relatively bigger by the thinness of the cheeks. But no!, the fancy dissolved like a transfiguration scene. This ugly little woman a tragic queen, Monkey Bewsher a hero, it was absurd.[2]

When the novel then ends, a few lines later, it is on this note of spiritual growth which Africa has forced on the white men, on the difference Africa has made to them. This is the Conradian bias, the crucial message of *Heart of Darkness*, as well as of *Lord Jim*, the moralist's version of the theme of imperial responsibility.

[1] Ibid., p. 229.   [2] Ibid., p. 239.

It is therefore useful to look briefly at the influence of Conrad on Cary before examining *Mister Johnson*, if only because in that novel also, Cary concludes his narrative with a reflection on the growth or education of his principal white character, Rudbeck. This influence has been generally recognised.[1] Arnold Kettle, speaking of Cary's career in the colonial service, called him a 'liberal imperialist', a phrase he had used for Conrad.[2] Andrew Wright has specifically mentioned *Heart of Darkness* as a novel which 'of all Conrad's works, surely . . . poses most centrally the question which Cary asks'.[3] Professor Mahood cites other patterns of influence. 'In many ways', she argues, *Mister Johnson* is 'an extension of what Conrad attempted in his short story. "The Secret Sharer". . . . The deep underlying affinity between Conrad's two men is expressed in their physical resemblance; in *Mister Johnson*, the same thing is indicated in similarities of temperaments.'[4] Cary, she adds, 'tries in *The African Witch* to match Conrad's creation in *Nostromo* of a whole state alive with dissension and treachery'.[5] In *Aissa Saved*, Cary insists on the need to 'get on with the job in the teeth of the world's injustice', the 'Conradian virtues of self-respect, self-reliance, of a proper pride'.[6] Professor Mahood further maintains that the experience Cary sought in his short stories was 'above all the Conradian one of self-discovery

---

[1] This interpretation of the Conrad/Cary relationship also seeks to correct Andrew Wright's argument (*Joyce Cary: A Preface to his Novels*, p. 73), that Bewsher is the Kurtz of *An American Visitor*.

[2] Arnold Kettle, *An Introduction to the English Novel*, vol. II (London, 1955), p. 184.

[3] *Joyce Cary*, p. 40.

[4] *Joyce Cary's Africa*, p. 117.

[5] Ibid., p. 146.

[6] *Joyce Cary's Africa*, p. 107. Professor Mahood does, however, point out that the final effect of *Aissa Saved* is different from Conrad's. The 'sensation' of reading the novel, she argues instead, 'is that of looking in a mirror and seeing only bone and muscle, the anatomy of life, whereas the experience we seek is rather that defined by Cary in his praise of Conrad: "life recognising itself"' (ibid., p. 106).

through novel situations and actions, the kind of incident described in . . . "Bush River"'.[1]

Cary himself acknowledged the influence of Conrad. In the Preface to *Aissa Saved*, he called Conrad, Hardy, James and the 'great Russians' his 'masters'.[2] In the *Paris Review* interview, he mentioned Conrad in particular among the 'lots, hundreds' who had influenced him. 'Conrad had a great deal [of influence] at one point. I've got a novel upstairs I wrote forty years ago in Africa, under his influence.'[3] Professor Mahood has identified *Daventry* as 'almost certainly' the novel referred to here. She suggests that although it gives 'a clear, pointed meaning to his recollections and intuitions', *Daventry* 'remains an immature work, and Cary's reputation would not be helped if it were published',[4] because it was 'connected with an earlier phase of Cary's African career' and 'reflects a state of mind from which he had to free himself to achieve anything as a novelist'.[5] How Cary could free himself from this influence we can see from his own reflections:

> I ask myself now why do I object to that—is it really bad, or is it because I'm prejudiced by something that's nothing to do with the book at all. Do I dislike that, because I'm a varsity man, or for anything I've been taught to believe, which is really affectation or prudery or snobbery, or prejudice, which I have allowed to stick in my brain unnoticed till its [*sic*] dangerous like a fungus, and is beginning to make my brains all mouldy.[6]

Eventually Cary did learn to 'shed the social prejudices of his earlier days in the colonial service'.[7] But another kind of 'prejudice' remained—a prejudice deriving both from a 'period' cult of Empire and of the white civilisation and from the influence of Conrad as a specific preacher of the virtues of

[1] Ibid., p. 17. [2] Preface to *Aissa Saved*, p. 10.
[3] *Writers at Work: The Paris Review Interviews* (New York, 1958), p. 61.
[4] *Joyce Cary's Africa*, pp. 89, 95.
[5] Ibid., p. 97.
[6] Letter of 10 September 1917, quoted in Mahood, *Joyce Cary's Africa*, p. 40.
[7] *Joyce Cary's Africa*, p. 40.

that cult. 'Bush River,' the theme of which Professor Mahood calls 'Conradian'—'self-discovery through novel situations and actions'[1]—offers good instance of the scope of this 'prejudice' and of its consequences for Cary's fiction.

Corner, the story's hero, loved the novel and the magnificent. He was in love with his black pony: 'Corner had never before owned a pony of such quality and he was obsessed with the creature. Indeed he had already committed a great folly for its sake.'[2] He was also in love with the Bush River. Corner found a certain attraction in all rivers and moving waters, but 'African rivers' in particular 'fascinated' him. As a soldier, Corner had other duties to perform apart from admiring river and pony. In fact he had instructions 'to avoid anything like a road or even a used track' (p. 11). Officers were indeed allowed their horses,

> but only in the main column—never on scout, point or patrol duty ... Corner's assignment was actually that of a man on scout duty all the way. But he had not been able to persuade himself to leave his darling pony behind in some horse lines to be neglected by strangers, starved by thieving orderlies, or borrowed by some subaltern for a forced march, to be left dying in a swamp' (p. 12).

These loves—for horse and river—come into conflict with his military duty. 'Corner knew his duty, but he said to himself that most of his course lay through high bush where a horse would be as easily hidden as a man.' He knew he was merely rationalising, for already the pony—called Satan—'had sent out a trumpet as good as a bugle call for every German within a mile' (p. 12).

Corner's romantic involvement with horse, river and adventure leads to the highly quixotic crossing of the river on Satan's back in spite of his sergeant's warning about crocodiles and Germans on the other side. 'He had no mind for anything but the river and Satan beneath him, who by means

---

[1] *Joyce Cary's Africa*, p. 17.

[2] 'Bush River', in *Spring Song and Other Stories*, Penguin Books (London 1963), p. 10. Page references to this story will be cited in parentheses after the text.

of the magnificent river, was going to achieve a triumph' (pp. 15–16). This quixotism is underlined. 'A man who chose to swim his own horse when a boat or a ford was available would have seemed quite mad; and if he managed to drown himself or his horse, he would also seem irresponsible' (p. 16). This judgement of Corner is only softened by the fact of Corner's youthful romanticism. At twenty-six, he was 'an extremely conventional young officer, a little bit of a dandy, a good deal of a cox-comb. He had a strong prejudice against the unusual,' but felt that 'he had to swim this river. He had a first class excuse for doing what he had often wanted to do' (p. 16).

Corner's crisis is not death or mishap but self-knowledge. Just as he crossed the river, he 'suddenly . . . heard a click and turned his head towards it. Over a bush, not ten yards away, he saw the outline of a head in a German soldier's cap, and a rifle barrel' (p. 18). The temerity of his action dawns on him.

> 'The Germans', he thought, or rather the realisation exploded inside his brain like a bomb on a time fuse illuminating a whole landscape of the mind. He was stupefied again by the spectacle of his own enormous folly, but also by something incomprehensible behind it and about it. And it was with a kind of despair that he said to himself, 'You've done it at last, you fool. You asked for it'. . . . He hadn't even a revolver, so he lay quite still, fatalistic, but not resigned. For he was resentful. He detested this monster of his own stupidity (p. 18).

When the shot for which 'he was holding his breath' did not come, he had 'a queer sensation so vivid that he still remembered it twenty years after, of floating lightly off the ground' (p. 19).

It is not with this theme of self-discovery, however that 'Bush River' ends. Corner's realisation of his 'enormous folly' and his final retreat from Satan and its admirers 'as if from contagion', yields to a theme which is more specifically Conradian. Rather than reflect on his own foolhardiness, Corner reflects on his good luck. 'Why had that German not

119

fired?' (p. 19). Corner is saved the burden of answering his own question. 'What was the good of wondering at chance, at luck, here in Africa? Next time it would be different' (pp. 19–20). This last sentence is an unnecessary, and even untenable, conclusion to the story as it is told. There is no justification in attributing any aspect of Corner's good fortune to his environment.

That this conclusion is nevertheless predictable we can see from an early passage in the story. African rivers, we are told, fascinated Corner. 'Looking at them he understood that old phrase "the devouring element"' (p. 10). The allusion to *Lord Jim*, even if misquoted, is nevertheless pertinent. It points to a different direction from that of the story's primary action; it attaches to the locale a destructive purposefulness which Corner could hardly be expected to overcome. If the 'element' Corner is in love with is 'devouring' then the conclusion of the story is logical. Corner's escape is only a miracle. 'Next time it would be different.'

We do not believe this conclusion because we do not accept the earlier Conradian identification of locale and fate. We are not encouraged to accept it, either, because, by 1945, Cary could hardly speak of the 'devouring element' in his own voice. By attributing it to Corner's romantic imagination, Cary makes the identification of locale and fate the personal opinion it ought only to be. The identification accordingly also becomes a possible 'criticism' of Corner's imagination. Corner 'asked himself how Africa survived against such destruction. At the same time, he thought how magnificent was the gesture with which Africa abandoned herself to be torn, like a lioness who stretches herself in the sun while her cubs bite at her' (p. 10). But when the story ends with the claim that this incident, the horse and the river were present 'all the more . . . to [Corner's] feeling, the feeling of one appointed to a special fate, to gratitude', we see that Corner's 'lucky' escape from the destructive element has become more important for the story than the taming (through experience) of his romantic disposition.

The discrepancy between the two purposes is a measure of that between the Carian and the Conradian modes. In the African novels (which are closest to Conrad's tales of exotic lands), Cary is caught between an exploration of a character —Corner's, for example—in which action and purpose, heroism and quixotism bring praise as well as danger, and a preference for mystery and the creation of a romantic determinism based on fidelity, honour and foreign lands. We can see that in 'Bush River' the Carian mode is more pervasive, and that the Conradian sticks out like the relic of an earlier story. Miss Mahood tells us that Cary was 'aware' by May 1919 'of the danger of his trying to see life through the spectacles of Conrad or of the Russians, instead of using his own eyes. Perhaps his awareness of this danger made him avoid reading contemporary novels during this tour.'[1]

Mister Johnson, Cary's last published novel of Africa, shows how far he had come towards eliminating the influence of Conrad and towards depending entirely on his own style. Johnson's story is, in the long run, the same as Corner's, only without Corner's good luck, and without Africa's 'devouring element'. Johnson, Cary says, is 'a young clerk who turns his life into a romance, he is a poet who creates for himself a glorious destiny'.[2] So, for a time, was Corner. Like Corner, Johnson felt he 'had' to do the things he did, the things 'he had often wanted to do. He told himself that he was not his own master, not in any sense of the word.'[3] When we speak of Cary's indigenous style prevailing over the alien Conradian style in the characterisation of Johnson, we are really saying that in the novel, Cary is able to give geography its due and incidental place in the action of the novel, and to attribute the interpretations of the world of the novel to the individual imaginations which create it. When we say that vestiges of

[1] *Joyce Cary's Africa*, p. 60.
[2] Preface to *Mister Johnson*, Carfax ed. (London, 1952), p. 5. Subsequent references to *Mister Johnson* are to this edition and will be cited parenthetically.
[3] 'Bush River', in *Spring Song*, p. 16.

I

the earlier Conradian inclination remain in *Mister Johnson* we mean that for all the 'everlasting pressure of the soul' on Johnson, it is on Rudbeck, not on Johnson, that the final burden of 'self-recognition' rests.

When Corner found himself within moments of death as a result of his folly, he learned his lesson. 'He detested this monster of his own stupidity.'[1] Johnson never recovers from his romanticism; or more properly, if Johnson ever came to a recognition of the distance between imagination and reality, he would have no 'inspiration' to grow 'ever more free in' (p. 227).

> Johnson knows then that he won't have to get up again from his knees. He feels the relief like a reprieve unexpected, and he thanks Rudbeck for it. He triumphs in the greatness, the goodness, and the daring inventiveness of Rudbeck. All the force of his spirit is concentrated in gratitude and triumphant devotion; he is calling all the world to admit that there is no god like his god . . . Rudbeck leans through the door, aims the carbine at the back of the boy's head and blows his brains out (p. 225).

In the very deliberate theatricality of this conclusion, we can see affinities with the end of 'Bush River' in the deployment both of styles and of themes. A predominating Carian vision, rooted in character and situation, suddenly yields to a Conradian complex seeking to use the life of the story for correlations quite incidental to it and only relevant to preoccupations about the burden of Europe. Rudbeck's burden rather than Johnson's tragedy becomes the novel's final concern. Having shot Johnson, Rudbeck 'answers obstinately, "I couldn't let any one else do it, could I?"' (p. 227).

This inclination to resolve the theme of his novel in the pattern of *Heart of Darkness*, the temptation to make the tragedy of a principal character the education of another, is Conradian; and Cary yielded to it for as long as he wrote about Africa. It is true, of course, that by 1932 when he published *Aissa Saved*, Cary had more or less mapped out a

[1] 'Bush River', in *Spring Song*, p. 18.

philosophy of life and fiction which was to sustain him throughout the rest of his writing career. Nevertheless, he was not immediately liberated from the obsession of a thesis-ridden and inflexible African theme. In his conversation with David Cecil, Cary spoke of the individual as 'a bit of universal Nature. But as an individual each man uses his mind and his imagination to create a world satisfactory to himself. That is to say, to satisfy his feelings, his affections, his ambitions, his hopes and fears, his family and so on.'[1] In the African novels Cary was only able to give this philosophy brief and fitful recognition. It is not until *Mister Johnson* that he gives it free rein.

Mister Johnson was published in 1939. A year later Cary published *Charley Is My Darling*. There can be little doubt, given this proximity of publishing dates, and Cary's habit of working on more than one novel at a time, that the emphasis on the creative and the moral imagination in *Charley Is My Darling* affected the final emphases in *Mister Johnson*. This is to say, in fact, that the sustained celebration of Mister Johnson's verve was positively encouraged by Cary's current interest in Charley. It becomes evident in such circumstances that *Mister Johnson* is not so much the last of the novels of Africa as the true beginning of Cary's later novels of the individual imagination. *Mister Johnson* thus stands as a bridge between the thematic and geographical necessities of the African series, and the metaphysical concerns of the later novels.[2]

Johnson, like Charley, is Cary's creative soul. He has imagination enough to seek to break away from both the constrictions of the native lethargy and of the mechanical

[1] *Adam International Review*, XVIII (November–December, 1950), p. 18.

[2] This is to qualify Wright's argument in *Joyce Cary*, p. 86, that 'in the characterisation of Mister Johnson, Cary moves in a new direction: he explores the destructive as well as the creative aspect of the free man'. In fact, after *Mister Johnson* Cary protagonists are unequivocally 'saved'. None of Cary's African protagonists is 'saved', except for Aissa and Johnson whose salvation is in any case equivocal.

routine of administrative life. After the harvests, the villagers around him revert to a holiday of hunting, dancing, singing, drumming, drinking and women. This is the good life for the average village man:

> At night he squats singing, their voices in his ear, their thighs touching his; he dances with the young men and the young girls spring and wheel before him. He knows them all, he has played with them from their babyhood, they know each other like brothers and sisters; they are like parts of one being and now every part is mad with the same frenzy, laughing at the same joke; feeling the same ache in their bodies. Their bodies are playing the same tricks, and while they jerk and leap, they burst out laughing at their strange appearance, their lewd inventions and their serious greedy faces. They fall into each other's arms with the same hungry rage and creep away into the dark bush among the rest; butting their heads at the scrub which stands in their way, weeping with indignation at the tic-tic which scratches their backs and swearing at each other when they bump in the dark.
>
> In the morning no one gets up till the sun is high and warm. Everyone has sore eyes, sore feet, sore heads and many bruised and cut all over. One has a torn ear, he does not know how he hurt himself. Another has a bite in his cheek, but he does not know what woman has bitten him or why. He lolls in the shade with a group of his friends, all sulky and languid. Some have strings tied round their heads to ease their headaches. The girls wander about in groups, with their arms about each other's waists, they too groan, feel their heads, show their cuts and bruises. But they are not so languid. They laugh among themselves and some of them telling a story of the night, sketch a dancing step. They have not drunk so much as the men and they are not so exhausted by love-making (pp. 155–156).

Johnson's imagination is too active to accept the easy routine of this life. Nor can it accept the tepid, even bored, lives of Ajali and Benjamin. Ajali 'alone behind the broad counter', 'like a scorpion in a crack, ready to spring on some prey', is 'obviously as bored as a reasonable creature can be; not to desperation, but exhaustion' (pp. 15, 16). Benjamin, the postal clerk, is caught in the meaninglessness of his presumptions to civilisation. When Johnson proudly announces his engagement, Benjamin 'a tall grave man of good education always dressed formally in dark clothes, says in his gentle voice: "I think sometimes I take a wife, but I think these native bush girls are so ignorant and dirty. It is not good till they have some educated girls"' (p. 30). He believes Fada to be 'a bad place for civilised people' and considers the 'civilisation' of its people 'too unequal' (p. 49). The fact is that he cannot create a satisfying world for himself out of the raw materials of actual life. When Johnson 'swaggers across the floor among the leaping, frenzied dancers in their exotic agony, to greet a new friend, Benjamin remains in his usual attitude of meditative distraction, his chin in the air, his eyelids half closed' (p. 133).

Johnson rejects the limitations of these lives. Fada may be 'primitive' but its women are 'well-known for beauty', and Johnson is poet enough to appreciate it—

> [Bamu] throws the pole, places the top between her breasts against the crossed palms and walks down the narrow craft.
> 'What pretty breasts—God bless you with them' (p. 11).

—and to celebrate it in song:

> *she smoot like de water, she shine like de sky.*
> *She fat like de corn, she swell like de new grass.*
> *She dance like de tree, she shake like de leaves.*
> *She warm like de groun', she deep like de bush* (p. 19).

These responses to Bamu's beauty are a spontaneous and total act of his whole self: the beauty he observes directly transforms his own being. 'You are so beautiful', he says to Bamu, 'you make me laugh' (p. 12). Excited by the prospect of marrying such a beauty—'she is fit to marry de King of Kano' (p. 31)—Johnson reacts with all the force of his imagination. With his morocco bag of letters under his arm, and 'his patent-leather shoes in his hand', he travels home (after his first meeting with her) 'at high speed, at a pace between a trot and a lope. In his loose-jointed action, it resembles a dance. He jumps over roots and holes like a ballet dancer, as if he enjoyed the exercise. But, in fact, his mind is full of

125

marriage and the ferry girl' (p. 13). He is late for work the next morning, and is 'in a panic'.

> But his legs, translating the panic into leaps and springs, exaggerate it on their own account. They are full of energy and enjoy cutting capers, until Johnson, feeling their mood of exuberance, begins to enjoy it himself and improve upon it. He performs several extra-ordinary new and original leaps and springs over roots and holes, in a style very pleasing to himself (p. 19).

Johnson finds romance not only in the beauty of Bamu, but even in his jobs as file-clerk at the station, as purchasing clerk in Gollup's store and as manager for Rudbeck's work-gang. At a period in the administration of the colonies when 'long views' were taboo, and zeal, 'above all, too much zeal' dangerous (p. 209), Johnson came to his dull tasks with enthusiasm and even bravura. He is thus able to talk Rudbeck into juggling with his accounts in order to be able to pay for the new road. At the same time, Johnson is able to make his position in the administration an opening to personal (not egotistic) glory. In Rudbeck's absence, Johnson *becomes* Rudbeck, and assumes all his power. He 'marches for a little while, passing from one [office] to another with an important air. He takes up the file baskets and says to the messengers, "Give way there." Adamu and his staff not only give way, they take the file baskets from him with polite bows. The procession to the clerk's office is a little triumph' (p. 56).

He goes even further, and gives the staff the day off. '"Mister Rudbeck excuses you."' For this they 'thank him with deep curtsies and go away. They know that Rudbeck has not authorised this holiday; they understand perfectly the complicated motives of good nature and glory which cause Johnson to give it; but they will, if challenged, look stupid and pretend innocence.' Meanwhile Johnson 'performs a little step-dance round the table, hums a tune', and as soon as the messengers are out of sight 'tries the safe' in the D.O.'s office, 'closely examines Rudbeck's table drawers, sucks at a spare pipe from one of them and goes through the pockets of his uniform'. This last action he could not help performing, for 'like other devotees, he cannot know too much, however trivial, about his idol' (p. 56).

Johnson's imaginative inventiveness enables him not only to survive the humiliation of his dismissal from the Government service but to prosper in the subsequent menial job he obtains as Gollup's agent. He faces the rudeness and the physical violence which Gollup periodically visits on his clerks, but he finds a way into Gollup's heart and into his till. While in Gollup's service, he becomes not only 'a renowned singer' but a 'very rich' man. He perfects a system of trading whereby 'he buys hides for himself in the compound and then sells them to himself in the store. For these hides he pays always top prices' (p. 136). When he, in turn, loses his job with Gollup and returns as Rudbeck's chief road-builder, he brings to his new post a similar devotion and enthusiasm and thus enables Rudbeck to complete his road within the limits of his financial resources and sooner than he had ever thought possible.

Johnson does not share in Rudbeck's long-term reasons for developing the road; but he can appreciate Rudbeck's attachment to it. It is as much to serve this 'attachment' as to satisfy his own desires for an active and satisfying life that he commits himself to the task. As in his other tasks, Johnson's sole aim is to secure the good life for himself and his friends, an aim well represented in a scene early in the novel. After Johnson had escaped arrest for his debts and survived Rudbeck's wrath,

> [he] goes back to the office and happily writes up the votes ledger. It seems to him now that he has not a single care in the world. Mr Rudbeck is his friend. The creditors have been put to flight. Moma appeased, he has the prettiest and most enviable wife in Fada, he will get an advance and a rise in pay, he will become the most important man, after Rudbeck, in the government (pp. 53–54).

The simplicity of this state of mind, when at rest, obscures its intensity and its single-mindedness in action. This intensity is, indeed, its strength and its weakness; it provides Johnson with the necessary momentum, but it does not allow him circumspection. In consequence, Johnson is oriented more towards the dramatic act than toward the calculated strategy. Enterprise becomes more important than achievment. When he steals from Gollup's store, he is (like Charley in *Charley Is My Darling*) more excited by the process of the theft than by the fruits of it. When he wants the keys to Rudbeck's safe, he would rather fight for them than have them offered to him. So 'excited' was he, in fact, 'by his own words and by the idea of the glory to be won in this difficult enterprise that he would be greatly disappointed if an earthquake were to crush the safe and a tornado blow the confidential reports into his hands' (p. 72). What Johnson's imagination lacked was discretion and direction, not energy.

He came close to recognising this during his days in jail. '"It makes you think,"' he says, referring to Saleh's disgrace, '"that a chap has to look out for himself—yes, you've got to be careful"' (p. 202). By the time of his execution, Johnson, again like Charley at his trial, is seriously confused, 'in the state of feeling often noticed in people before a dangerous operation' (p. 225). In this state, Johnson cannot evaluate his past conduct. Apprehension of danger, 'at a certain point of intensity, like a boiling kettle, becomes still, but all the quickened powers of the soul pursue their favourite task, with exaltation' (p. 225). Thus, like Charley, Johnson is not 'reformed', but is 'confirmed' in his own idealism. Deriving peace—'lightness and cheerfulness'—from the certainty of his death, he seeks 'to do or say something remarkable, to express his affection for everything and everybody, to perform some extraordinary feat of sympathy and love, which, like a statesman's last words, will have a definite effect on the world' (p. 225). But Johnson can have nothing extraordinary to say. His tragic end, like Charley's term at a rehabilitation centre, is one more conclusion to the encounter of two realities: one an objective world of constants, the other a subjective world of individual creativeness. As with Charley, Johnson's life, not Johnson's success, is his vindication.

But though Mister Johnson is, like Charley, a youth of imagination, it is important that we also see him in his proper place as a *demi-evolué*, 'a mission-educated African who has passed out of tribal society and into government service'.[1] Several interpreters of the novel have indeed concentrated too much on this aspect, and Miss Mahood justly chides them for it.[2] Yet, she herself concludes that in *Mister Johnson*, Cary came to see in the 'creative freedom' of Africans ('who live in the minute, improvising new songs and new dance rhythms') a force to match the 'freedom of self-reliance based on knowledge' which the 'Kiplingesque white man had to give Africa'.[3] It is evident, therefore, that Cary's handling of the character of Johnson must be assumed to amount to the author's comment on the hero as the victim of a conflict of cultures. This judgement is implicit in the differences between Charley and Johnson; in the fact, for example, that Charley is not automatically overwhelmed by the lure of gold in the same way that Johnson is by aspects of European life.

The fact is, of course, that Johnson's imagination, if seen as part of an 'African' imagination, is assumed to be only too naturally excited by the attractions of an alien culture. One of Cary's models for Johnson, as the Preface tells us, had written letters home 'full of the most wonderful yarns for his people on the coast. He was always in danger from the Germans (who were at that moment two hundred miles away); he was pursued by wild elephants (who were even further away from our station); he subdued raging mobs of "this savage people" with a word' (p. 5). In these letters, Cary recognised the same turn of mind as he was to find in Charley's boasting. Charley would tell 'lies' not so much to deceive his playmates as to sustain the reputation for experience and daring which he had suddenly acquired. Similarly

[1] Douglas Stewart, *The Ark of God*, p. 141.
[2] Mahood, op. cit., p. 170. See also Wright, *Joyce Cary*, p. 84, and Arnold Kettle, *Introduction to the English Novel*, vol. II, p. 179.
[3] Mahood, p. 196.

Cary's letter-writer made himself out as 'a hero on the frontier' whereas he was actually 'a junior clerk in one of the most peaceful and sleepy stations to be found in the whole country' (p. 5). Neither the reference to Germans nor the talk of 'savages' has any necessary relevance, however, to any clash within him between Europe and Africa; neither Europe nor civilisation excites him, but a natural desire to indulge his pride and his imagination.

The Johnson who results in the novel is less independent of the clash than this. We see him at first caught in the worship of Bamu, 'a local beauty, with a skin as pale and glistening as milk chocolate, high, firm breasts, round strong arms' in a region whose young women 'are well known for beauty' (p. 11). Of the two forces which control his subsequent conduct—the attraction of Bamu, and the attraction of white civilisation—it is the latter to which he pays more insistent court. The result is that his offer of marriage to Bamu virtually amounts to an attempt to 'save' her from her environment. '"Oh Bamu, you are only a savage girl here— you do not know how happy I will make you. I will teach you to be a civilised lady and you shall do no work at all."' '"You don't know how a Christian man lives"' (pp. 11–12). In his imagination Johnson dresses Bamu up in several changes of 'blouse and skirt, shoes and silk stockings, with a little felt hat full of feathers' (p. 13).

This enthusiasm is fed by an admiration for European civilisation more than it is by Bamu's beauty. It is true that Johnson knows he will be 'envied for that beautiful girl', but this is not as important to him as the prospect that he 'will not only make her a civilised wife; he will love her' (p. 13). Thus, whereas Cary's romantic letter-writer was only indulging his fancy with the 'idea' of fighting Germans, elephants and savages, Johnson is using his imagination in a different way— to pursue the beauty of a European or 'civilised' existence. The beauty which he apprehends is, predictably, only a paltry version of the real thing. In the tradition of the *demi-evolué*, his 'idea of a civilised marriage, founded on the store catalogues, their fashion notes, the observations of missionaries at his mission school and a few novels approved by the S.P.C.K., is a compound of romantic sentiment and embroidered underclothes' (p. 13). The clerk's romanticism is still a poet's romanticism; it belongs to those who care to create 'glory' for themselves. Johnson, as we saw, has a great deal of this romanticism. The other romanticism—that of the worshipper of the store catalogue—is the restricted romanticism of the 'half-educated native'. It arises apparently only when a starved but creative native mind is in love with the paraphernalia of civilised life. Thus the absurdities of Johnson's marriage ceremony, for instance, are both a product of his search for glory, and his close identification of that glory with mission rituals and mission underclothes.

The attractiveness of a character sharing in these two distinct romanticism—the one ennobling, the other naïve—is difficult to account for. Some critics have, indeed, seen Rudbeck's tragedy as that of a 'promising' colonial officer 'forced by Negro love, naïveté, and distress to an act of unpremeditated tenderness and regard. It is purely personal and fleeting.'[1] If Mrs Rudbeck's response is any clue, it is evident that Rudbeck's respect for Johnson's imagination was essentially a kind of patronage. Celia Rudbeck who, in Cary's early drafts, was to have been a rather unpleasant person, is shown in the novel as taking to Johnson much as her husband had done. Privately she calls him 'Mr Wog.'

> Rudbeck hears her laughing at six in the morning and asks.
>   'What's the joke, darling?'
>   'Only Mr Wog.'
>   'He's a comic, isn't he?'
>   'A perfect quaint.' (p. 92).

The pet-dog image is certainly relevant to the view of Johnson as the native worshipper of a culture he cannot comprehend; for it provides a parallel for what must necessarily have been an unequal relationship. Arnold Kettle has been

[1] Bloom, *The Indeterminate World*, p. 59.

criticised for pointing out this dog–master relationship in the novel. Rudbeck, he says, 'shoots Johnson as he would shoot a suffering dog to whom he feels a special responsibility, and although the horror of this act is conveyed, it is somewhat blunted by the underlying paternalism of Joyce Cary's own attitude'.[1] One need not accuse Cary personally of paternalism to see the duality of Johnson's existence as poet and *demi-evolué*, and the possibility of a genuine as well as a paternal relationship with his European admirers. For one cannot unequivocally admire or even respect Johnson's miserably absurd notions of European civilisation without being paternalistic.

Cary had used the dog–master parallel in another story involving Englishmen and Africans. In 'A Touch of Genius', Robbins is the unusual Englishman who marries a Nigerian girl; his household includes an elderly Nigerian cook and Jiso, a young girl of fourteen who serves as a general hand around the house. 'Robbins gazed at [Jiso] with the pondering expression one sees sometimes on the face of a dog-owner.'[2] Significantly, Robbins, now that his wife has deserted him, plans to take Jiso along with him to his mining expedition up the plateau. The other Englishmen, in surprise, ask whether he was actually taking her along.

> Robbins looked round them with his most amused expression. He shouted at last. 'Well, I ask you, gentlemen, am I taking 'er or is she taking me—I ask you, gentlemen . . .' He pointed at Jiso who, at once, like a dog which has learned a trick and performs it on all inappropriate occasions, went down on one knee. But this time, sure that she was doing the right thing, she grinned broadly.[3]

Rudbeck's relationship with Johnson is, of course, more

---

[1] Arnold Kettle, op. cit., p. 183. He has been criticised by Mahood, p. 170 and Bloom, p. 56.

[2] 'A Touch of Genius', in *Spring Song and Other Stories*, p. 297.

[3] Ibid., p. 297. See also p. 283, where Jiso's and Bamu's love for Robbins is compared to that of dogs. 'I suppose nobody loves so strong as a dog—and that's funny thing, too. . . . Why should an animal love a human being.'

complicated and more subtle than this between Robbins and Jiso. It is nevertheless important that we recognise that because of his unbounded passion for civilisation, Johnson is more than liable to the patronage of those he imitates, and that this makes him thus incapable, as in his relationship with Major Gollup, of telling those who respect him from those who just 'like' him.

> I don't mind to kill you, ole chap, 'cause I 'gree for you too much. I've known enough niggers by now, all sorts and both kinds, and I always say they aren't 'arf as black as they look if you treat 'em right. Naow, and some of the real hugly ones like yourself, the real wogs, isn't the worst, neither. . . . A chap may be a nigger—that the way Gawd made 'em—same as 'e made warthogs and blue-faced baboons —'e can't 'elp being a nigger—but 'e can 'elp being a man (p. 125).

Johnson is nigger enough to boast of his 'frien' Gollup' (p. 130). Indeed, he is 'carried away, not merely by friendship, but by something in the air, the exciting sympathetic spirit of the occasion which is like a real party, a drum party. . . . In that exciting atmosphere of gin and poetic sympathy which belongs only to artists and drink parties, Gollup and Johnson often pursue their own creations simultaneously' (p. 128). Since Gollup's Sunday night 'corroborees' are nothing but bestial, the identification of Johnson's creativeness with Gollup's drunken conduct is obviously a diluting of the quality of that creativeness. To think otherwise would be to 'patronise' him.

On the one side, then, Johnson's *alter ego* is Rudbeck, on the other, Major Gollup. Both men expose the two principal forces in the *evolué's* existence, idealism and naïveté. In *The African Witch*, these two features produce a tragic complex in Aladai and Coker. In *Mister Johnson*, they produce a blissful and (subsequently) a pathetic effect on the hero. Mister Johnson is so carried away by the transcendence of his own pursuit of civilisation that he is incapable of self-appraisal, and consequently of self-analysis.

In his encounters with Bamu and Bamu's family, the comedy of this idealism is mainly at Johnson's expenses. To

133

his earnest protestations of prestige and civilisation, Bamu is indifferent. She says nothing, 'pays no attention', 'does not even look at him' and is even 'slightly annoyed by his following her, but doesn't listen to his words' (pp. 11, 12). When he 'suddenly stops, laughs and kisses her', she 'pays no attention whatever. She doesn't understand the kiss and supposes it to be some kind of foreign joke' (p. 12). To his inspired comment that, like Mrs Rudbeck, Bamu was 'now a government lady' and must learn 'civilised behaviour', Bamu simply replies: 'My brother Aliu has a bad toe' (p. 57). She refuses to wear the cheap 'mission' clothes Johnson ordered for their wedding, and insists on wearing her native dress to meet Mrs Rudbeck.

> 'You're not one of the savage bush girls any more. You're as good as a white woman. That's why I give you a cloth fit for a government wife.'
> 'What's he say?' Bamu asks.
> Falla aims her pestle at the mortar. 'I don't know—something about the chief.'

After his fight with Gollup, Johnson rushes home to Bamu to brag about it. '"I knock Mister Gollup down so that he was like dead. An' the judge come with the police."' Bamu is not impressed. She 'shuts her eyes again'. He continues to tell her of his plans to leave for the south where Bamu 'shall have that motor car like a big Lagos lady'. To all this Bamu 'says nothing' (p. 141).

Bamu is not alone in her attitude to Johnson's extraordinary enthusiasm for civilisation. Bamu's brother, Aliu, 'a tall, powerful man of about thirty' not only did not admire Johnson's bravado, he found it odd. When Johnson so rashly announces his intention to marry Bamu ('"I'm clerk Johnson. I'm an important man, and rich. I'll pay you a large sum. What's your name?"'), Aliu is properly puzzled. He 'scratches his ear and reflects deeply, frowning sideways at Johnson. He can't make out whether the boy is mad or only a stranger with unusual customs' (p. 12). When Johnson persists in offering a rather high price for Bamu, Aliu and his companions are 'visibly startled. Their eyebrows go up. They gaze at Johnson with deep suspicion. . . . The village children come and stare. The general opinion is that he is mad' (p. 13). The settlement which he reaches with the brothers in exchange for Bamu is, not surprisingly, more than he can ever pay. Since Johnson is already in debt, his immature and irresponsible display of power and wealth in the pursuit of civilisation is justifiable only because of the blissful, lyrical (and precarious) happiness which it offers him. Hence the complexity of Ajali's response. It is true that Ajali is 'perishing of boredom' and that in consequence, 'the follies of the new clerk are as exciting as scandal in any country village. They fill his empty mind with ideas and his empty time with a purpose' (p. 16). Yet he is realist enough to see that Johnson was ignoring the 'constants' of life, and that Johnson could not escape the consequences of this folly indefinitely. When Johnson tells him the terms of his marriage contract—'"Six pounds down and pound a month for ten month'—very cheap"'—Ajali asks him simply: '"But, Mister Johnson, can you pay six pound?"' (p. 31).

There is indeed jealousy and malice in Ajali's mind when he contemplates the prospect that Johnson might be dismissed from his job. '"Oh dear! What going to happen to dat poor Johnson now?"' (p. 19). But his reasoning is not unjustified. 'A friend of mine,' Cary relates in *Art and Reality*, 'as a child, thought he could fly, and jumped off the roof. Luckily he came down in a flower-bed and only broke a leg. . . . He affronted a law of gravity, a permanent part of a reality objective to him. . . . Wrong ideas about gravity or the wholesomeness of prussic acid are always fatal.'[1] Basing his fear for Johnson on a similar idea, Ajali is naturally 'astonished' at the boy's 'triumph'. It seems to him that Johnson 'defies the very laws of being; and still goes unpunished. It is most unjust' (p. 196).

What turns Johnson's blissful existence in defiance of the 'very laws of being' into the pathos of his last days in his

[1] *Art and Reality*, p. 19.

inability to organise and direct his own exuberance. The novel tells us that Rudbeck and Johnson had the 'power of refusing to notice unpleasant things, until [these things] force themselves upon [them]. This gives [them] much happiness and many sudden depressions' (p. 78). This is more true of Rudbeck than it is of Johnson. Rudbeck, for example, continues to postpone the execution of Johnson until the very last minute. But, unlike Johnson, he does contemplate the unpleasant things even if he does not immediately face them. Johnson, on the other hand, seems not only unwilling to confront the unpleasant, but even incapable of contemplating them. He does have a strong imaginative sense of the possibilities of failure, but this ability is uncritical, and accordingly, its response is absolute. He can see himself, a stranger in England, threatened with eviction by a British Prime Minister for misconduct: '"He drunk, he play de fool, he black trash. He no care for nobody"' (p. 37). But he can also find a glorious way out of the predicament:

De King, he say, oh no, Mr. Primminister, don't do so, I know dat Johnson from Fada, he my faithful clerk from Fada (p. 37).

This escape is, obviously, a gift from Rudbeck, a gift Rudbeck makes in appreciation of Johnson's devotion to him in Fada. It would thus seem that Johnson built much of his personal assurance on the expectation of Rudbeck's intervention. That is to say, he felt freed from the obligation to take care of himself by the thought of Rudbeck's friendship which he believed he had secured through devotion and self-sacrifice. 'Affection, self-sacrifice', Cary says in the Preface, 'are very common things in this world. . . . But so is daylight, and yet we do feel a special moment of recognition . . . at every sunrise' (p. 6). 'Remembered goodness', Cary claims in dedicating the novel to Musa, 'is a benediction'.

If Johnson's uncritical exuberance is linked with his worship of Rudbeck and of 'civilisation', it is not surprising that he does not develop mentally into recognising the world's real proportions, that he does not grow out of his naïve romanticism. This is, in fact, the cause of his unfortunate fall. Even after the murder of Major Gollup, Johnson still thinks Rudbeck will let him off because of their friendship.

> 'Doesn't make any difference,' says Dog-nose. 'Not if you've killed a man.'
>
> 'He's been good to me.'
>
> 'It's the law. If it says you've got to be hanged, why he'll have to hang you, see?' (p. 206).

At his trial, Johnson continues to celebrate his connection with Rudbeck in a genuine expectation that a reprieve would come. 'He opens his mouth to greet [Rudbeck], but, seeing Rudbeck's judicial pose of gloomy air, he thinks that perhaps it would be unwise. He therefore stands silent, effacing himself as much as possible behind the constable while the court arranges itself' (p. 207). Because Rudbeck is in the last resort powerless to grant this reprieve on the basis of friendship, and because he knows that Johnson has built his fantasy of a world on this friendship, Rudbeck is caught in a miserable dilemma. He goes away 'still more depressed and resentful against the mysterious enemies that close him in, regulations, conditions of the Service, and luck, whatever they are. It's more bad luck that Johnson should ask for something impossible' (p. 215).

There can be little doubt that the 'inspiration' in which Rudbeck was 'growing ever more free' and which seemed 'already his own idea', was the inspiration of remembered goodness, of Johnson's total confidence in the saving power of his God and King, Rudbeck. Such an inspiration is present in Cary's Preface which tells of the clerk who stayed up all night to copy a report because 'he did not want me to "catch trouble"; that is, to get a reprimand for being late with my quarterly reports' (p. 7). What this clerk demonstrated, 'so suddenly and unexpectedly' was 'not only a power of devotion but the imaginative enterprise to show it' (p. 6). This clerk differed in many respects from Johnson, but Cary says he 'remembered him when [he] drew Johnson. . . . It is not true that Africans are eager but fickle. They remember friendship quite as long as they strongly feel it' (p. 7).

These two sides of Johnson's 'mode of being' are necessary for any generalisation on the achieved meaning of *Mister Johnson*, the meaning which the novel succeeds in conveying. From the point of view of Johnson as a man of imagination, his death, like Charley's detention, implies no judgement of the quality or the validity of that life. His triumph is self-created; his death in the tradition of romanticism, is not defeat, but merely cessation. From the point of view of the other tradition, of course, Johnson is their hero, not because he is imaginative, but because he is imaginative enough to presume to the glory of their civilisation.

Because Johnson belongs to these two traditions the final meaning of his career cannot be stated in simple terms. Johnson may be Blake's 'terrible boy', the 'image of God who dwells in darkness of Africa'.[1] He does indeed give 'life to Rudbeck' in 'regions of dark death'. But is he Orc, the sublime and revolutionary fire-brand of Blake's *America*, whose fires force the forests 'into reptile coverts' and 'play around the golden roofs in wreaths of fierce desire/Leaving the females marked and glowing with the lusts of youth?' Johnson's death may be laid at the door of the colonial administration, but he is not the victim, as Hoffmann argues, of 'white man's laws, in a white man's world of legal justice, [where] there is no question of leniency'.[2] He is not a 'living condemnation of his white superiors', as others contend, any more than Charley is a condemnation of a civil society. Nor can we ignore the naïve side of his life and hold with Christopher Fyfe that the 'world has been changed by the creative force Johnson represents—courageous, forward-looking and dynamic'.[3] For Johnson only exemplifies the creative imagina-

---

[1] See Mahood, *Joyce Cary's Africa*, p. 185.

[2] Hoffmann, op. cit., *South Atlantic Quarterly*, LXII (Spring, 1963), p. 243.

[3] Christopher Fyfe, 'The Colonial Situation in *Mister Johnson*', *MFS*, IX (Autumn, 1963), p. 230.

tion, not the creative intelligence. Finally, though we recognise the liberation which he brought to his life and to that of Rudbeck, we need not go so far as to credit Johnson with 'the mastery to shape his own life and even to shape its close'.[1]

Because the significance of Johnson's career is complicated in this way by his two modes of being, the meaning of this novel is poised between the celebration of Johnson's imaginative vitality and the capacity for devotion on the one hand, and on the other, the portrayal of the burden which his naïve devotion to European values places on Rudbeck, the representative of those values. The need to attend to these two demands is responsible for the shift at the end of the novel from Johnson's coming to terms with reality to Rudbeck's growth through the ordeal of executing his protégé. 'All the force of [Johnson's] spirit is concentrated in gratitude and triumphant devotion; he is calling all the world to admit that there is no god like his god. He burst out aloud, ' "Oh Lawd, I tank you for my frien Mister Rudbeck—de bigges' heart in de world" ' (p. 225). Immediately following this, Rudbeck shoots him. Rudbeck does not 'feel any violent reaction', nor is he 'overwhelmed with horror', but rather he feels 'a peculiar relief and escape like the man who, after a severe bilious attack, has just been sick' (p. 225). The effect of this crucial end on Rudbeck is clearly only emetic, not cathartic. It is almost as if, faced with the difficulty of a concluding idea,[2] Cary had grabbed a typical Conradian device and so made *Mister Johnson* the story of Rudbeck's education rather than that of Johnson's magnificent existence.

[1] Mahood, *Joyce Cary's Africa*, p. 186.
[2] See Mahood, p. 186, for a brief examination and evaluation of Cary's earlier versions of the final scenes.

6: Conclusion

By 1931, when *Aissa Saved* was published, Cary had been away from Africa for over ten years, during which period he maintained hardly any link with Africa or with his fellow administrators in the Colonial Service. This isolation, Miss Mahood notes, 'was all to Cary's advantage as a novelist' because 'it gave a peculiar sharpness and clarity to his recollection of events' and enabled him 'to achieve "aesthetic distance" and so create a world apart'.[1] One should note, however, that by this time, also, Cary had changed a great deal as a man and a thinker. For one thing, he was now concerned with the study of the nature of man himself and the nature of political and moral order. For another, he was no longer satisfied with the pseudo-Darwinian view of society which had encouraged his first attitudes to colonial politics. Now, in 1931, he had ceased to have the same kind of interest in colonial and even in British politics, *per se*. Cary had changed from the administrator to the metaphysician. 'I had forgotten politics,' he wrote of that period, 'I was deep in other studies, in philosophy, history and letters.'[2]

These studies led Cary into a more fundamental reconsideration of the nature of political order and of human freedom and he found himself propounding what, in *Power in Men* (1939), he called 'a new state theory'. It is this concept of freedom that he was to extend to the African scene in *The*

[1] Mahood, *Joyce Cary's Africa*, p. 187.
[2] *The Case for African Freedom and other Writings on Africa*, Austin, 1962, p. 14.

Case for African Freedom (1941).[1] The influence of the personal experience obtained during his African service is very much in evidence in the booklet, but Cary was not counting on that experience for the truth of his point of view.

> I do not write as an African expert who has given life to African problems, but as a man who, in his African service, made mistakes, who afterwards reflected on that experience and its meaning; who after ten years of active, thoughtless, and various experience in the world, began, rather late in youth, to ask what it amounted to; to dig up all his foundations, to find out exactly what they were; who discovered, then, as you might expect, that some of them were mud, some were hollow caves of air, others sand; and who then slowly and painfully rebuilt them, as far as he could manage the task, as a coherent whole, on which to found a new life and a new mind.[2]

The ideas about order and freedom which emerged from this rethinking and study may be justly said to be basically existential. Man, he now holds, is 'not a political or economic animal' and is often 'moved by sympathies, tastes, faith, which have nothing to do with politics or cash, and he is ready to fight for them'.[3] Indeed, men are 'living souls' who are prepared to 'ignore even the primary needs of their bodies for some ideal satisfaction; glory or learning, religion or beauty'.[4] For this reason, the goals of political freedom, like those of all other forms of freedom, are bound to be individual and particular. 'In any political question, I ask first, how does this affect the real man on the ground, the people in their private lives?'[5] Yet, the need for a harmonisation of goals and the elimination of conflicts demanded an institutional kind of authority. Hence, though 'man rebels in his heart against all authority', yet 'at least in his heart', he

---

[1] 'When I was asked three years ago to write about Africa, I said "I have not been in Africa for years, and I am busy with other things"; but the publishers answered, "You have a certain point of view about politics . . . If your views apply to Africa, let us have them."' *The Case for African Freedom*, p. 14.

[2] Ibid., p. 14.

[3] *Power in Men*, Seattle, 1963, p. 35.

[4] *The Case for African Freedom*, p. 132.

[5] Ibid., p. 12.

asks for 'justice, and opportunity which only authority can secure to him'.[1] In that paradox lay the fundamental and inevitable untidiness of the world of politics and order. 'To try to make the world safe for anyone is as hopeless a project . . . as to command that everyone shall think alike . . . that storms shall stop blowing and earthquakes cease to crumple.'[2]

Such views do not date easily and they go beyond the specific problems of the colonial Africa that Cary knew or the one that developed after him. Their universal application meant, in any event, that the African scene was included in this philosophical generalisation and that the problems of political order could not be different in Africa from what they are in Europe and elsewhere.

Cary, himself, has given some account of his loss of interest in politics as government and of the growth of his interest in this 'science' (of politics) which he said was also 'half-art, half-metaphysic'[3] and which concerned itself with 'living souls' seeking 'some ideal satisfaction'. Cary links this change in his thinking with that crucial period of his life (1920–32) when he tried to acquire 'a new education in ethics, in history, in philosophy' in order to be able to 'reconcile the mechanism of the scientific idea and the free creative soul of the world'.[4] Cary found an answer in Kant's philosophy where the two realms of necessity and freedom meet in the moral consciousness of man,[5] and in Kierkegaardian existentialism which allowed for the 'solitude of man's minds' as well as 'the unity of their fundamental character and feelings'.[6] It was

[1] *Power in Men*, pp. 37–38.

[2] 'Sources of Tension in America', *Saturday Review*, 23 August 1952, p. 35.

[3] *The Case for African Freedom*, p. 12.

[4] Quoted in George Steinbreacher, 'Joyce Cary: Master Novelist', *College English*, XVII (May 1957), p. 389.

[5] See F. Copleston, *A History of Philosophy*, vol. VI, New York, 1960, p. 392.

[6] See *Writers at Work: The 'Paris Review' Interview*, ed. Malcolm Cowley, New York, 1958, pp. 57–58, where Cary calls himself an existentialist 'in the school of Kierkegaard', not 'in Sartre's sense of the word'.

not till the two great trilogies that Cary was able to give expression in fiction to this idea of human life and politics. But the idea would certainly have been of interest to him during the years when he was working on the African novels. It did certainly help give the characters of those novels that reckless Carian élan and that uncompromising faith (in ju-ju, Christ or tin-prospecting) which were to be their undoing. At any rate, it is clear that the evolution of this idea of man as an independent soul alive with his own compelling passions and ideals was a necessary prerequisite for Cary's emergence as a novelist. Until then, as Cary himself said, he could not 'even write dialogue'.[1]

It would also have been impossible for Cary to mature as a novelist without that crystallisation of his aesthetic ideas which followed his resolution of the philosophical dilemma of mechanism and freedom. *Art and Reality*, his lectures on the creative process, were delivered at Cambridge in 1957, but the ideas developed in them are in keeping with the philosophical implications of his earlier political tract, *Power in Men*. In fact, both arise from the same source. The arguments which led him to move from the empiricism of the Utilitarians (Hume being their primary authority) to the transcendental idealism of his political theory also led him from the view of art as the expression of intuition to a view of it as a simultaneous and complex expression of feelings *and* concepts. The argument is ultimately Kantian: works of art are 'propositions for truth' whose validity 'can be decided by their correspondence in logic and experience with the real'.[2] Rejecting Croce's equation of intuition and expression, Cary argued that the artist had to find the 'symbols' to 'fix' his intuition (the 'subconscious recognition of the real') which is necessarily evanescent—like 'a flash between two electric poles'.[3] The true work of art, then, is a construction

---

[1] Quoted in Steinbreacher, op. cit., p. 389.
[2] *Art and Reality: Ways of the Creative Process*, New York, 1961, p. 20.
[3] Ibid., p. 28.

which offers us 'truth in a context' which is made 'actual, complete and purposeful to our experience'.[1]

The direction of such ideas as these, as can be expected, is away from the limited significances of the traditional foreign novel of Africa. For these ideas transcend race, place and time. They reach out to those constants of the human mind and human life which give identity to the variousness of individual and group conduct. They lead in *Charley Is My Darling* to that engrossing portrait of the young delinquent which becomes the study of the growth of moral consciousness in childhood. In the first trilogy, they encourage the celebration of the eternally symbolic virtue of the lives of Sara and Jimson and to the intellectual assertion of this virtue in Wilcher's pilgrim ideal. In the 'political' trilogy, these ideas lead Cary to his philosophical examination of the nature of political order through a record of the careers of a politician, a housewife and a soldier.

These ideas are also behind Cary's African novels, as the main chapters of this study have suggested. But they are not given full scope because of the baggage of 'fact' which Cary brought home with him from Africa by way of journal letters and drafts and out of which, for nearly a decade, he sought to fashion a satisfying work of art. In speaking of the 'peculiar sharpness and clarity' of Cary's recollection of the events of his African experience, Miss Mahood remarks that Cary 'could at any time confirm [these recollections] by looking up his journal-letters'.[2] Far from being an unqualified asset, these journal-letters and early drafts, written when Cary was still caught up in 'the chilvaric ideals of a latter-day imperialism'[3] and as yet unsure of his own views on anything, were, in fact, a liability. For they represented, not simply a record of his African service but also an interpretation of that experience from a specific cultural standpoint. That is to say, the African experience which Cary

---

[1] *Art and Reality: Ways of the Creative Process*, New York, 1960, pp. 155, 191.

[2] *Joyce Cary's Africa*, p. 187.   [3] Ibid., p. 17.

recorded in his letters and drafts was shaped by the cultural assumptions which, at that point in history, were as public as they were personal. The voice is that of the Representative Englishman and the incidents recorded belong to the life of a white-man-in-Africa. No novel philosophical view of life and no fundamentally unique understanding of the events encountered shaped these records. Cary wrote in his own character—which accounts for the captivating authenticity of his narratives. But that character was not different enough or knowing enough to amount to more than just Cary's expression of a more or less conventional point of view.

This is a limitation which, later, was also to affect *A House of Children* by imposing on it the burden of recollected attitudes, as if the recollection was in itself a sufficient theme. It is a limitation, also, which we find in *Castle Corner* and in *A Fearful Joy*, two novels which read like correct period sketches but lack that interior significance which comes from a fresh and compelling theme or idea. Hence, the narrative and the attitude become inseparable one from the other with the result that the authorial voice is inevitably implicated in the imperial condescension of the times:

> They madden me sometimes when I am very busy, and have a dozen [cases] waiting to be heard—by starting like this, 'I never tell a lie. I would not dare to tell a lie to the white man, the powerful one. I know it is no good (What's your name? from me), God prolong your life, O King, Lord of justice (What's your name and what do you want?). I thank God that you are ruler of the land'—and so on. The compliments take few minutes—the business two. . . . Especially as the most complimentary tell the biggest lies.[1]

In a passage like this one taken from the letters, it is the high comedy of the white man's burden rather than the meaning of these encounters that Cary recaptures. It is this same kind of self-satisfied comedy that we find in *Castle Corner*, the same imperial view of the African scene from a point outside and above it.

[1] Quoted in Mahood, *Joyce Cary's Africa*, p. 51.

145

Jingler sang [Jarvis'] speech. . . . Jarvis, during Jingler's speech, lowered his nose, scratched it, glanced at the map with affectionate longing, and pursed up his lips to whistle, but recollecting himself just as Jingler finished, unpursed them again and continued, 'On the other hand, chief,' he paused and half turned to Jingler. 'Also will do. The great white queen sends me, her servant Jarvis, to offer to you her friendship and protection that you and your people may also enjoy peace and safety which you certainly need. . . .

Jarvis at once walked up to the chief, took his hand and warmly shook it. The cries of rage which were now sounding on all sides of the clearing were changed to a deep murmur of horror. The chief of Laka's hand is never touched.[1]

Killam groups *Castle Corner* with those novels which, he argues, reveal 'in a variety of ways, but with a consistently high artistic success, the essentially selfish motives of imperialism'.[2] If indeed *Castle Corner* is that kind of novel, the comedy of the passage just quoted does not support its purpose. For, eventually, even though they take on the aspect of light-hearted and irresponsible dare-devilry—Killam calls it 'foolhardy bravery'[3]—Jarvis' adventures are still imperial in a respectable sense. They may mock the seriousness of the old administrators, but they show with what little effort the young white man could manage to cow a people and extend the empire.

In 1918, Cary would have been interested in a novel that told that kind of story. The elaborate notes and sketches about Castle Corner were tailor-made for just such a novel. In the late '20s Cary would not have been interested in such a story. Rather, he would have turned to the philosophical implications of the imperial event; he would have wanted to represent the meaning of that period of history, to do for colonial Africa what he was to do later in *To Be a Pilgrim* for post-Edwardian England. Cary did not do this. He did not, one suspects, partly because the sketches from Africa were already there to use, and partly because he could not really

[1] *Castle Corner*, London, 1952, pp. 174–175.
[2] Killam, op. cit., p. 82.
[3] Ibid., p. 82.

change his world and write completely outside the tradition of the novel of Africa. To be able in the 1920s to use his African journals and sketches as a basis for his fiction without carrying over with them some of the limitations in point of view and understanding characteristic of his years in the colonial service, Cary would have had to re-live his African experience in the light of a new metaphysics, learn to separate his former attitudes from his accounts of episodes and depend entirely on his critical intelligence for the re-appraisal of the message of his six years' experience in Africa.[1]

We must, then, say that Cary's novels of Africa represent the compromise that was the result: a compromise between the pull of a new view of life which Cary was developing and the pull of the tradition of the foreign novel of Africa to which his early drafts belonged. In this sense, these novels occupy a unique place in the history of the foreign novel of Africa as well as in the history of Cary's career as a novelist. They are certainly not his best work and his reputation as an English novelist cannot depend on them. They are neither the embodiment of his best ideas nor the culmination of his art as a novelist. Yet as these essays have tried to suggest, these novels form an important part of the story of his actual importance as a novelist. Specifically, they give him a special place in that long and undistinguished line of European novelists of Africa as one very much concerned not only with Africa but with the processes of art. It is in the nature of the ideas about life and art with which he tried, belatedly, to transform his experience of Africa into works of art, that we have to look for an explanation of whatever distinction there is in his African novels.

[1] See *Joyce Cary's Africa* (pp. 89–104), for an account of Cary's unfinished novels of Africa, *Daventry* and *Cock Jarvis*.

147

Bibliography

Adam International Review, XVIII (November–December 1950).

ALLEN, WALTER, *Joyce Cary*, London, 1954.

ARDREY, ROBERT, *African Genesis*, London, 1967.

BARBA, HARRY, 'Cary's Image of the African in Transition', *University of Kansas Review*, XXIX (Summer, 1963).

BLOOM, ROBERT, *The Indeterminate World: A Study of the Novels of Joyce Cary*, Philadelphia, 1962.

CAIRD, EDWARD, *The Critical Philosophy of Kant*, Glasgow, 1909.

CARY, JOYCE. *Aissa Saved* (1931), London, 1952.

—— *An American Visitor* (1932), London, 1952.

—— *The African Witch* (1936), London, 1951.

—— *Castle Corner* (1939), London, 1952.

—— *Mister Johnson* (1939), London, 1952.

—— *Power in Men* (1939), Seattle, 1963.

—— *The Case for African Freedom* (1941), Austin, 1962.

—— *Art and Reality* (1958), New York, 1961.

—— *Spring Song and Other Stories*, London, 1960.

—— 'Sources of Tension in America', *Saturday Review*, 23 August 1952.

CAXTON, WILLIAM, *Mirror of the World*, ed. Oliver T. Prior, Early-English Text Society, Oxford, 1963.

COLLINS, HAROLD R. 'Joyce Cary's Troublesome Africans', *Antioch Review*, XIII (Fall, 1953).

CONRAD, JOSEPH, *Youth, Heart of Darkness, The End of the Tether*, London, 1967.

COPLESTON, F. *A History of Philosophy*, vol. VI, New York, 1960.

COWLEY, MALCOLM (ed.), *Writers at Work: The 'Paris Review' Interviews*, New York, 1958.

CRISP, DOROTHY, 'For King and Country', *Saturday Review*, London, 10 June 1933.

DAICHES, DAVID, *The Novel and the Modern World*, Chicago, 1939.

ECHERUO, MICHAEL J. C., '*Robinson Crusoe, Purchas His Pilgrimes*, and the "Novel"', *English Studies in Africa*, X (September 1967).

FORESTER, C. S. *The Sky and the Forest*, London, 1948.

FORSTER, MALCOLM, *Joyce Cary: A Biography*, London, 1968.

FRENCH, WARREN G. 'Joyce Cary's American Rover Girl', *Texas Studies in English Literature and Language*, II (Autumn, 1960).

FYFE, CHRISTOPHER, 'The Colonial Situation in *Mister Johnson*', *Modern Fiction Studies*, IX (Autumn, 1963).

GARY, ROMAIN, *The Roots of Heaven*, London, 1960.

HOFFMAN, CHARLES G., 'Joyce Cary's African Novels: "There's a War on"', *South Atlantic Quarterly*, LXII (Spring, 1963).

—— *The Comedy of Freedom*, Pittsburgh, 1964.

HUNTER, J. PAUL, 'Friday as a Convert: Defoe and the Accounts of Indian Missionaries', *Review of English Studies*, n.s. 14 (1963).

KETTLE, ARNOLD, *An Introduction to The English Novel*, vol. II, London, 1955.

KILLAM, G. D. *Africa in English Fiction, 1874–1939*, Ibadan, 1968.

KILPATRICK, FLORENCE, *Red Dust*, London, 1926.

Lagos Weekly Record, Lagos, Nigeria, 1892–1896.

MAHOOD, M. M. *Joyce Cary's Africa*, London, 1964.

MELVILLE, HERMAN, *Redburn, His First Voyage*, New York, 1957.

MUIR, KENNETH (ed.), *Elizabethan and Jacobean Prose, 1550–1620*, Pelican Book of English Prose, vol. I, London, 1956.

New Statesman and Nation, London, 16 December 1933.

OBIECHINA, E. N., 'Through the Jungle Dimly: European Novelists on West Africa', *Literary Studies* (Punjab, India), I (Fall, 1970).

RAMSARAN, J. A., *New Approaches to African Literature*, 2nd ed. Ibadan, 1970.

STEINBREACHER, GEORGE, 'Joyce Cary: Master Novelist', *College English*, XVIII (May, 1957).

STEWART, DOUGLAS, *The Ark of God*, London, 1961.

WOLKENFELD, JACK, *Joyce Cary: The Developing Style*, New York, 1968.

WOODCOCK, GEORGE, 'Citizens of Babel: A Study of Joyce Cary', *Queens Quarterly*, LXIII (1956).

WRIGHT, ANDREW, *Joyce Cary, A Preface to His Novels*, London, 1958.

Index

Italic figures indicate principal references in text